D1243837

PHILOSOPHY IN
REVOLUTION

Philosophy in Revolution

by HOWARD SELSAM

GREENWOOD PRESS, PUBLISHERS
WESTPORT, CONNECTICUT

Library of Congress Cataloging in Publication Data

Selsam, Howard, 1903–
  Philosophy in revolution.

  Reprint of the ed. published by International
Publishers, New York.
  Includes index.
  1. Dialectical materialism. I. Title.
 ₁B809.8.S39 1976₁   100   75-36103
ISBN 0–8371–8619–6

© by International Publishers Co., Inc. 1957

Originally published in 1957 by International Publishers, New York

Reprinted with the permission of International Publishers

Reprinted in 1976 by Greenwood Press,
a division of Williamhouse-Regency Inc.

Library of Congress Catalog Card Number 75-36103

ISBN 0-8371-8619-6

Printed in the United States of America

CONTENTS

FOREWORD

COUNTLESS BOOKS have been written on the great social conflicts of our time. Many concern themselves with the theoretical or philosophical differences that both underlie and express these conflicts. None, to my knowledge, has attempted to analyze the way these very struggles are transforming thought itself.

Walt Whitman once wrote: "Never were such sharp questions asked as this day." He was right then, and would be even more right today, for the questions people are asking in their thought and implying in their actions challenge the whole body of mankind's traditional outlook on the world and on the meaning of life. It will be useful to explore some of these questions in the light of man's historic struggle to understand nature and himself.

The great issues of our time—democracy, peaceful co-existence of opposed social systems, colonial liberation and self-rule for all peoples, the employment of science for a rising standard of living for the whole world, public ownership and control of production—are reflections of the most sweeping social transformation mankind has ever witnesssed. Not sufficiently recognized is the fact that the very process of this social transformation must inevitably bring with it the greatest and most far-reaching intellectual or ideological revolution of all history. In the famous words of Karl Marx and Frederick Engels, this is man's movement from "the Kingdom of Necessity to the Kingdom of Freedom." In philosophical terms, it is man's movement from all forms of mythology and superstition to a scientific materialist world-outlook. This outlook is rooted in his knowledge of the world and in his growing capacity to master physical nature and social relations for the fulfillment of his hopes and aspirations.

It is admitted on all sides today that Marxism challenges all traditionally accepted modes of thought. The Marxist outlook, created out of the struggles of the modern European working class on behalf of that class, has become a world-wide theory for the emancipation of all oppressed and submerged groups and classes. As such, it constitutes a veritable revolution in thought. As it is grasped by millions in their struggle for peace and prog-

7

ress it is transforming man himself and revolutionizing all his concepts concerning the nature of the world and his place in it.

We have here two distinct but interconnected propositions. The first is that Marxism, as a body of philosophical principles and a social science is not just another philosophy and another theory of society. It is a radical departure from the previous forms of both, and thus revolutionizes our outlook on the world and our whole historically evolved approach to all questions of man's nature, freedom and goal. It is, of course, at the same time, built upon all that was scientific and progressive in previously developed thought.

The second proposition is that in struggling for national liberation, progress and socialism, the people come to embrace Marxism or to accept its leadership, and in the process change themselves and their world outlook along with their social conditions. In these struggles for liberation from all forms of oppression and exploitation man has to build new social relationships. In doing this he is transforming himself ideologically, is bringing to an end the old established forms of philosophical and religious outlook, and is creating a totally new understanding of himself and his world.

HOWARD SELSAM

CHAPTER I

PHILOSOPHY AND SOCIETY

IT IS NOT the purpose of this book to introduce social conflicts into philosophy but to show that philosophy is inseparably connected with social conflicts. To say that philosophy is partisan to one or another grouping or class in times of social ferment is not to deny philosophy or to negate its value. It is rather to show that it has, and always has had, genuine relevance and meaning for the problems of men and women. From ancient China, India, Greece and Rome to the present day, philosophical discussions have reflected social issues, and major philosophical arguments have reflected and referred to vital and significant social struggles.

Most philosophers, however, have thought that their philosophy was a product of "pure reason" and would be degraded by any admission that economic or political interests had intruded themselves. Rather is it the other way around. Philosophy has meaning and value because it deals with social questions, takes sides with regard to them, and relates them to general theories of the nature of the world and of man.

One of the deplorable by-products of the philosophers' own illusions concerning their divorce from social problems and class alignments is the popular notion that philosophers are people with their heads in the clouds. The ordinary person thinks he cannot understand the philosophers and need not "trouble his poor head" about them. Philosophers have mistakenly sought to give the appearance of being removed from social classes and their influence. The masses have countered by seeking to remove themselves from philosophy. But neither separation is possible. The fact is that, of necessity, the great class struggles of the age of imperialism constitute at the same time the greatest philosophical, or ideological, struggles of all history.

The subject matter of philosophy has consisted historically

of precisely those questions which are (1) of the most vital concern to human beings in the solution of their life problems, and (2) are not apparently resolvable on the basis of either everyday experience or available scientific knowledge. Just about everyone on earth, from adolescence on, has some views about at least some of these questions. The people called philosophers are simply those who have devoted themselves to a serious examination of them.

But what are these questions one calls philosophical? They are such as these: What are we here for? Where did we come from? What is the world all about? Expressed somewhat more concretely they are: Was the world created or has it existed eternally? Do things happen for a purpose and through a plan or do they come about through the operation of natural law? Was the world made for us or are we just products of its development? Is there a life after death or are we just here and when we die we're dead? Do all things change or are they fixed and eternal? Is the world real or could it be just a dream? Do we perceive the world through our senses or is it beyond their reach? What is good and what makes anything good? What is mind? What is matter? What is the relation between the two? These are the questions people have asked about the world from the beginning of civilization, and such is the stuff of philosophy.

The above questions may not at first seem to have particular social significance. Yet the answers to them provide the basis for the answers to a host of other questions that directly concern human life, forms of social organization, and principles of action. A few examples serve to reveal this. Is this earthly life our only one or is it merely a prelude to a heavenly life? Has God ordained all that will happen or is our future in our own hands? Can we have such knowledge of the laws of nature and society that through the mastery of them we can plan and control our future, or is our knowledge necessarily limited and our future beyond rational control and unpredictable? Can human nature change or are the basic forms of character and behavior forever fixed? Can men and women cooperate for the common good or is it always a question of each for himself? Are we all "brothers under the skin" who can live together in equality and peace or is the "white race" predestined to rule the world? Is something good because God commanded it or because it satisfies human needs and interests? Do the ideas of leaders or the struggles of the masses move society forward? These are basic questions of our time and the answers to them are dependent upon the answers to those stated earlier.

There have been, indeed, many other questions people have asked about the world and which philosophers have discussed. Some have fallen into disuse, through changes in social institutions and resultant intellectual habits, such as whether reason or revelation is the source of knowledge. Others, such as whether air, fire or water is the basic stuff of which all things are made, or whether the species of animals were all separately created or evolved from simple forms, have been superseded by positive scientific knowledge. The disappearance of a host of problems for the second reason accounts for the relatively high degree of "technological unemployment" among philosophers. Areas over which many loved to argue have been removed forever from their purview by the advance of science. In fact, one of the theses of this work is that the end of the class struggle will allow for a scientific answer to all these questions and thus revolutionize philosophy, as we have known it. Meanwhile these questions and the different answers to them reflect the positions of different groups and classes in modern society, as they have done through the ages.

Often enough professional philosophers do not know that these are their problems. They belittle their own profession and trivialize their thought, as we shall see in subsequent chapters. But the whole of historic philosophy, with the exception of Marxism, is built on a particular philosophical presupposition that became, with some philosophers, almost an "occupational disease." In its most extreme form it is the idea that the world exists in order that the philosopher might know and contemplate it. It is more commonly found in the notion that material production exists for the sake of intellectual production and is subordinate to it. Different forms of social-economic relations cause this idea to express itself in different ways, but common to all is the idea that society is properly and necessarily divided into the masses of people who do the physical work of the world and those who, freed from all manual labor, direct and organize the labor of others and do society's intellectual work. This has indeed been the chief justification for the existence of ruling classes through the ages. Another of the theses of the present work is that with the industrial revolution and the rise of the modern working class there is no longer the slightest justification for this division of manual and intellectual labor and that society not only no longer needs but can no longer tolerate the division of itself into two such parts.

Meanwhile the old religions, the mythologies and superstitions of past ages, are losing their sway over the minds and hearts of countless millions. This is not to say that people have consciously broken with the prevailing ideas or have achieved a new world-outlook. It means that whether they are American working-class Protestants, Catholics or Jews, Latin American or Italian Roman Catholics, Iranian and Indonesian Moslems, or Indo-Chinese Buddhists, they are being led, by the circumstances of their lives, to believe in struggle rather than submission, in the primacy of housing, jobs, food, and social-economic equality over all promissory notes on heaven, in the right of all to a share in the good things of the earth, including education and culture, rather than in the right of any privileged class, sect, or nation to possess everything. It becomes ever clearer that as the whole non-socialist world is increasingly divided into exploiters and exploited, into those who want war and those who want peace, those who seek only ever greater profits and those who struggle to keep their families together in elemental decency, so does this division become expressed in philosophical or ideological terms between outmoded superstitions and mythologies and an objective materialist approach to the problems of life.

Today two points of view are in conflict whether the contestants are conscious of it or not. A coal miner or a steel worker may not know that he has a fundamentally different outlook from the mine owner or the steel bosses, but let it become a question of wages, hours, safety devices, or union security, and the two classes at once part company. For the former the question is: How can my family live? How can I be protected against accidents? How can I keep from being worn out and dumped on the scrapheap in the prime of my life? For the latter the only question is: How can I get a higher return on my capital investment, how can I achieve maximum profits? Behind it is the old, old story: production for the aggrandizement of those who own the land, tools, machines, or production for the well-being of all who produce.

This struggle now cuts across national boundaries, as never before, and has become a world struggle. It has acquired a totally new dimension through the fact that world capitalism has been in a state of general crisis for nearly forty years, scores of millions in the capitalist and colonial countries alike challenge the dominant values, and one-third of mankind has already turned its back on capitalism and is at work building a totally new order of society.

It is not an accident but a product of historical necessity that this struggle is reflected in the highest levels of ideology, that is, in philosophy and ethics. It divides them into two kinds—the philosophy and ethics of the working class, of the exploited and oppressed everywhere, and the philosophy and ethics of the imperialists, the exploiters. Included among the latter, of course, are their many agents in exploitation, both those who derive their livelihood from managing capitalist enterprises and the political apparatus capitalism requires, and those who derive theirs from perpetuating, defending, and purveying capitalist philosophy, ethics, and ideology generally. This class division in the realm of ideology or thought is so basic and profound, that one of the principal tasks of the "thinkers" of the exploiting class is to deny that there is any such division. Such philosophical schools as pragmatism and positivism have as one of their prime conclusions that there are no classes and no class conflict. Denying any class struggle, the ideological agents of the capitalist class must deny any class division in the realm of ideology. They are then free to deny any class partisanship on their part and to insist blithely upon their sublime objectivity and angelic aloofness.

A few hundred years ago, similarly, there were two kinds of philosophy—that taught in the "Schools" by the "Schoolmen" and that of the rebels, the spokesmen of the rising capitalist class, who were invariably outside the universities. The issue then was that of a narrow, dogmatic scholasticism—functioning as the handmaiden of theology and designed to maintain the feudal system—against an approach created to reveal new truths and to liberate life, the arts, and sciences from the dead hand of the church and the land owning feudal nobility. Only spe-

cialists today know the names of the scholastics of the sixteenth
and seventeenth centuries who opposed the rising tide. Many
have heard of the martyred Bruno, and of Bacon, Descartes,
Spinoza, Hobbes, and Locke.

Today, again, two kinds of philosophy are in mortal combat.
But it is not now a class of merchants, traders, manufacturers,
and their intellectual representatives that is challenging the ruling class and fighting for political power. Whole nations, vast
masses of hundreds of millions of people, are struggling to get
out from under the yoke of bondage. This is the greatest social
revolution known to mankind. It is the movement from the rule
of a minority of oppressors to the rule of the working class and
broad people's forces representing the interests of the overwhelming majority. Its goal is the transition from class to classless society. And it includes an intellectual revolution of prodi-
gious proportions. As Marx and Engels said in the *Communist
Manifesto,* "The communist revolution is the most radical rupture with traditional property relations; no wonder that its development involves the most radical rupture with traditional
ideas."

It is the purpose of this book to demonstrate certain basic
and simple ideas concerning the nature of philosophy, its history,
and its place in the world today. Central is the question of
what philosophy is and the nature of its development through
the ages. The two popular and mutually contradictory bourgeois views are (1) that philosophy is a mere succession of individual opinions concerning the nature of the world and of man,
and (2) that philosophy is the "love of wisdom" and that its
history is the history of the development of man's knowledge
and understanding of the world.

Neither of these views is satisfactory. The history of philosophy is more than a succession of individual world outlooks.
Such a view ignores the social forces that inspire and shape
philosophical thought, and fails to recognize the influence of
specific stages of scientific and technological progress. Further,
it fails to see any logic in the pattern of philosophical development itself. On the other hand, the history of philosophy is not
the same as the development of man's knowledge of his world.
Otherwise it would be identical with the history of science,
which is assuredly not the case.

This problem is resolved once we view philosophy in its actual historical development in class society. Then we find that from its beginnings in the ancient world to the present day it has been characterized by a struggle between the proponents, however bold or timid, consistent or wavering, of a scientific materialist world outlook and those of a religious, mystical, idealist world-view. Indeed, the central thesis of this work is that the true historical meaning of philosophy and its central significance is found in this struggle for a materialist outlook against all opposite tendencies.[1]

From this approach five propositions, which constitute the basic themes of the present work, may be formulated as follows:

(1) The history of philosophy is the history of the struggle of man for a scientific materialist world-view against all forms of idealism and obscurantism.

(2) This struggle reflects the class struggle and is inseparable from it, with progressive classes emphasizing and developing materialism and reactionary classes holding onto and embellishing idealism. The rising capitalist class made especially great progress towards a materialist world outlook and laid a basis for the later Marxist revolution in philosophy.

(3) All philosophy, however, prior to Marxism, regardless of the class it represented and hence regardless of its relatively progressive or reactionary character, was the expression of a small intellectual elite, removed from direct participation in the processes of production. This fact left an indelible and inescapable imprint on both the form and content of philosophy and prevented it, even in its most progressive stages, from solving certain central problems, especially those pertaining to the relation of mind and matter, the origin and extent of the knowledge process, and the nature of the good life.

(4) Marxism, as the position of the modern industrial working class, brought about a complete revolution in philosophy because it was based on the standpoint, for the first time in history, of the actual producers, and because it is the outlook of a class that, once it became conscious of its position in society, struggled for the elimination of all classes and of all exploitation. Thus as a class it has a different relation to the world of nature and of society and requires only a scientific approach to all questions. It can solve questions left unsolved by previous philosophy.

(5) With Marxism and its consistently materialist and dialectical world outlook the historic goal of philosophy begins to be realized and its place increasingly taken by the natural and social sciences and the generalizations of logic and dialectics. This is not to say that there are no unsolved problems but that the solution of all problems can and must be sought through scientific investigation rather than by philosophical speculation.

From its beginning philosophy has been a participant in the class struggle. It has been partisan to a progressive or a declining class and thus has sought to advance science or to advance superstition. Just as animism and magic characterized primitive communal life so has philosophy characterized class society, from the fifth and sixth centuries B.C. in ancient China, India, and Greece to the present day. It made great progressive leaps forward in the hands of a progressive class in one place and time, only to have such gains challenged by new reactionary and obscurantist movements such as represented by Platonic idealism, Berkeleyanism, and by the pragmatism and positivism of our own day. If so much of traditional philosophy has been concerned less with the mastery of nature by man through science and technology than it has been with the instrumentalities for the control of man by man, it has been given this problem by class society. And finally, the very nature of class society with its division of manual and intellectual labor, inevitably left its mark on philosophical thought in the form of abstractness, and of remoteness from the actual problems of people, the problems of production, the problems of man's material and spiritual well-being.

The aim of this volume is to develop, with the minimum possible technical detail, the general theses that have been stated. It will seek to reveal more concretely the richness of the philosophical thought of Marx, Engels and Lenin, as well as to show the effect upon all of mankind's current struggle for colonial liberation and socialism. The socialist transformation of society will not come as a change in man's economic and social relationships alone, nor as mere quantitative changes in productivity. It will transform man himself and his total outlook on the world. This change is, as Mao Tse-tung has said, "none other than the complete overturn of the world of darkness . . . and its transformation into a world of light that never existed before."

In proceeding further, however, we need to examine certain assumptions and implications of the view that the history of philosophy is the history of the struggle of mankind towards a scientific materialist world outlook. To hold such a view, as Marxists do, is to take philosophy with utmost seriousness. It is to say, for one thing, that philosophy is not merely part of the superstructure of one or another form of class society. It is to dismiss any "debunking" of philosophy, such as is common in some bourgeois circles, as simply another manifestation of the prevailing anti-intellectualism. It is to treat philosophy as meaningful and relevant to science and social life because it is part, even in its negative aspects, of man's historic struggle to interpret the world in which he lives and to secure his place in it.

The Marxist view of the history of philosophy takes as significant its great traditional questions: Is there a God? Is there life after death? What is the purpose of life? It has been recognized, even in hostile circles, that Marxism does have this respect for the examination of these questions. As the Catholic philosopher, Jacques Maritain, wrote, "And even Marxist atheism, however absurd we may think it, supposes at least, that human reason must answer the question whether God is or is not, without seeing refuge in the parentheses of a science of phenomena, from which it refuses to emerge."[1] Marxism also makes short shrift of views, only too popular in petty-bourgeois intellectual circles that social struggles and movements are merely "practical" and don't need philosophical theorizing.

Another significant result of this Marxist approach is that it does not see historical or contemporary thinkers in terms of their sincerity or their moral motives, or any other purely subjective factors. Rather, it sees them in objective terms of social and class relations and commitments, of the specific stage of the development of the sciences and technology (and philosophy), and in terms of particular levels of development of the class struggle. Concretely, this means seeing them not in terms of good or bad men but in terms of their total world outlook and their ideas of what life could and ought to be. How did the philosophers look upon the various classes of people around them? Did they like people and trust them, or did they fear the masses? Could they envision another kind of class relation—

not to mention the elimination of classes—or were they so committed to given relations that nothing else was conceivable. Plato, for example, could see no possibility of change, while Aristotle at least left the possibility open when he said, "If every tool, when summoned, or even of its own accord, could do the work that befits it . . . if the weavers' shuttles were to weave of themselves, then there would be no need either of apprentices for the master workers, or of slaves for the lords."[2] The point is that philosophers were and are people, sharing a social, cultural, and economic life. If their class is good, that is, has a future, can develop the forces of production, they are good. It is not a question of sincerity, of abstract virtue, but of class orientation. And this in turn must be seen not in terms of what class one is born into but with what one identifies oneself: in which class the individual finds his life's purpose or meaning. Superfluous from this point of view are questions such as: was Plato sincere? Did he really believe that rulers must systematically lie for the people's good? Did Hume believe that thorough-going scepticism was the best foundation for Christian orthodoxy, or did John Dewey really believe that for people to believe something is for it to be true? The question concerning Hume's denial of causality or Bertrand Russell's denial of the validity of proper names, including that of "Bertrand Russell," reflect neither the philosopher's insincerity nor his foolishness, but the objective dilemmas of his class. Did Alexander Hamilton believe that the people is a beast? Surely he did, but if that is possible then any irrationality is equally so. He was no more or less sincere in this than was Plato or John Dewey. An objective approach asks only what class did they belong to and affiliate themselves with, and what role did this class play at that particular time in social development. Thus when we find anything so preposterous as the denial of causality and the objective world we must see it in terms not of a philosopher's absurdity, or as it is done often enough in terms of the absurdity of philosophy as such, but in terms of a class that has no future.

If the conservative side dominates the history of philosophy that is because until 1917, conservative classes have dominated history with relatively short periods of revolutionary ferment in between. Leibniz's "the best of all possible worlds," is not a joke in the history of philosophy. It is simply the candid statement of the basic premise of the dominant ruling class tradition. It is the justification of the existing order, the sanctification of things as they are. And when it is opposed, as it was by Voltaire in his *Candide*, it is only because a new class is arising that thinks it can manage the affairs of society better. Or, again, the reigning objective idealism is opposed by the subjective idealism of positivism and pragmatism when in the rise of imperialism a more clever and timely disguise is required to cover up the sharpening class struggle.[3]

The conservative character of the major part of classic philosophy was clearly expressed in our own country during the past century. The first philosophy periodical to be published in this country, the *Journal of Speculative Philosophy* (1867-1889), carried on its masthead: "Philosophy bakes no bread but it gives us God, freedom and immortality." Philosophy, in other words, has nothing to do with our mastery of this world but only with our salvation in another. And the freedom it gives us is that freedom from materialism and science which today passes under the name of pragmatism and positivism. The current situation in American philosophy is so bad that one eminent philosopher, Ralph Barton Perry, has written: "Philosophers themselves have trivialized philosophy. In scepticism they have lost their nerve. Through emphasis on the cult of resignation they have made philosophy the opium of the intelligentsia. . . . They have sold their birthright for a mess of positivism." This is a justifiable commentary on the dying stage of ruling class philosophy.

Philosophers themselves admit that the status of philosophy in our colleges is a sad one, so much so that during the years of World War II the American Philosophical Association undertook, with Rockefeller money, an examination of the subject. This examination took counsel not only with members of the profession but also with poets, newspaper editors, lawyers, clergymen, business men, government officials and others. Conversations with workers and trade unionists are not mentioned. There was a general consensus that something was wrong and that "something ought to be done." The commission labored and brought forth a report, entitled *Philosophy in American Education*. They said that they brought into contact, among other things, "the campus with Wall Street." They complained that "there is not in our contemporary situation an authoritatively accepted body of doctrine called 'philosophy' for which duly accredited spokesmen can pretend to speak." The commission never dreamed of inquiring why this is the case, of trying to seek out those forces, pressures, and conditions in the capitalist world which prevent agreement on a scientifically oriented world view. On the contrary, speaking of the "greatest philosophers" the report says: "they can see beyond the familiar things and the present human culture, and even civilization itself, to ultimate reality and destiny—and this gives them a kind of authority indeed, that has no limitations of time, place or society."[4] Such a mystical approach to philosophy can only serve to turn away from it, with contempt, all rationally and scientifically oriented students.

All the factors that have been discussed give contemporary bourgeois philosophy its own special character—that of being something between previous superstition and subsequent unimpeded science, whether favoring the one more than the other. It was left to Bertrand Russell to define philosophy appropriately, even if not appreciating the full implications of his own definition. He wrote: "Philosophy, as I shall understand the word, is something intermediate between theology and science."[5] That is precisely what classic philosophy has been in the main. Even the materialist Epicurus did not abolish the Gods but only banished them. Plato and Aristotle frankly required them for political purposes. Philosophy has been something intermediate between theology and science, now more one, now more the other, depending on the nature of class relations and the exigencies of the particular situation. Mostly the philosophers kept a weather eye open for the day when a few Gods, a little bit of a God, or a very, very remote God, or just the name "God," might not be a good thing for the friends of "peace and order." With the exception of Diderot and d'Holbach in eighteenth century France, who among the philosophers dared stand unequivocally against religion in any form? As spokesmen of actual or potential exploiting classes they could not take a clear and firm position. Too often they have had their feet in worlds wide apart, somewhat like the 28 believers with assorted ailments who in 1948 took off for the shrine at Lourdes, France, in a Constellation—using this amazing product of modern science to fly back to the Middle Ages and primitive magic.

W. T. Stace, in his work on Hegel, is a little afraid at one point in his introduction that the philosophy he is depicting sounds altogether too weird for any credence. He writes:

> That the entire existent world is appearance may seem at first sight to be a conclusion repugnant to the common sense of humanity. It may be well, therefore, to show here that philosophy is not divorced from the common beliefs of mankind. For this very doctrine makes its appearance popularly in the religious consciousness. From Christianity we understand that God created the world, but that God himself is uncreated and primordial. This means that God owes His being to nothing other than Himself, and is therefore real, but that the world owes its existence to God, who is the source of its being, and is accordingly an appearance.[6]

This is, incidentally, an unsolicited endorsement of Engels' statement that the great basic question of all philosophy is: which comes first, thinking or being, mind or matter—did God create the world or has it existed eternally? It also confirms his observation that Hegel makes world creation very much more difficult than does Christianity.[7] But what precisely does Stace do in this passage? He takes as a standard the "common sense of humanity," exactly as do the clergy and theologians who argue that there must be a God because of the common consensus of mankind's opinion. Then he shows that Hegel does it more subtly, with greater sophistication, that he is simply expressing in a non-religious form the basic idea of all religion.

The textbooks of the history of philosophy reveal without the slightest embarrassment the essence of the traditional academic approach. Here it is brought down to the lowest common denominator in the interests of pedagogy; here it is stated without the frills and ornamentation of the system-builders. One of the old standbys is that of the German, Alfred Weber. His definition of philosophy and its relationship to science reads:

> Philosophy is the search for a comprehensive view of nature, an attempt at a universal explanation of things. It is both the summary of the sciences and their completion; both general science and a speciality distinguished from science proper; and, like its elder sisters, religion and poetry, forms a separate branch among the manifestations of the human mind.
>
> The different sciences have special groups of facts for their subject matter, and seek to discover the causes of these phenomena, or to formulate the laws according to which they are produced. In philosophy, on the other hand, the human mind endeavors to rise beyond such groups

and their particular laws, and to explain the world as a whole, or *the universal fact or phenomenon,* by the cause of causes, or the first cause. In other words, it attempts to answer the question, Why does this world exist, and how does it happen to be what it is?[8]

Such a conception of philosophy holds that (1) it is a special manifestation of the human mind (whatever that means), born of, or at least the younger brother of religion and poetry, (2) it "completes" the sciences and is above them, and (3) it explains *everything* in one fell swoop, or at least attempts to.

Weber, in his *History of Philosophy,* shortly after the passage quoted above, drew a conclusion concerning the relation of science and philosophy. "True science," he wrote, "and true philosophy have always been in perfect accord, and though there may be a semblance of rivalry, their relations are today as harmonious as they can be.[9]

There are so many things factually and theoretically wrong with this sentence that it is hard to begin distinguishing them. If science and philosophy had always been in perfect accord philosophy would have been superfluous. Philosophy served rather to regulate and to delimit the sciences, seeking to keep them within such bounds that they would be unable to challenge traditional viewpoints whose origin lay in religion. Secondly, their relations today are harmonious only because for the last seventy or so years the only influential philosophies having any contact with the sciences whatsoever have so trimmed their sails as not to oppose anything the sciences have established, while denying that science can tell us anything about objective reality. "We," the philosophers say, in effect, "will claim to know nothing you scientists do not find to be the case, if you will admit that all you are doing in your science is to organize, most economically, your sense data, and do not pretend to know anything about a reality independent of and objective to you." This is the school of Machism, logical empiricism, pragmatism, that arose relatively simultaneously near the end of the last century in Austria, Germany, France, England, and the United States. One of its most vocal representatives in this country today, Philipp Frank, Professor of the Philosophy of Physics at Harvard University, who had the distinction of being criticized by Lenin, (in his *Materialism and Empirio-Criticism,* in 1908), explains perfectly frankly that this school of philosophy saved science from its enemies—by denying that it was knowledge of any objective reality.[10] He is even so broadminded as to admit that dialectical materialism ("diamat," he calls it), would be a good philosophy for science if it avoided "the description of matter as something existing objectively."[11]

Jacques Maritain, the philosophical spokesman of "liberal" Catholics, perfectly well understood the meaning of this "harmonious" relation of science and religion when he wrote of positivism or the Vienna School that it "leaves the door open to faith (on condition that it should not be a knowledge) and to theology (on condition that it should not be a science)."[12] He says further of positivism, "to link science to a general atheistic conception, or to speak of a 'scientific atheism,' is from its point of view pure nonsense. In this it is drastically opposed to other tendencies . . . and especially to the philosophy of science proposed by dialectical materialism."[13]

This is not a pretty picture, but a picture it is nonetheless. It is a picture of bourgeois philosophy at its own dead end, an end in which it repudiates its own earlier radiant claims to know the world. Like the thought of previous defunct exploiting classes it is content to help prevent science from destroying superstition and to prevent science from being applied to the problems of society. It is dialectical materialism as the philosophy of the working class which alone carries forward the one great idea of progressive historical philosophy, the idea, namely, that through our sense experience and reason, by the methods of the sciences, we humans can know ever more about the nature of things, and so knowing, achieve ever greater mastery of our world.

The working class is led by its position in society, its needs and interests, its struggles for better conditions, to seek to eliminate all false and unscientific ideas, from those about the Gods to those of a future life and of the inequality of races and the sexes. It suffers defeat every time it fails to take a scientific materialist position. Only when it is led and guided by its distinctive class philosophy, dialectical materialism, is it assured of success. Just as it learns that it cannot emancipate itself without emancipating all mankind, it also learns that it cannot emancipate mankind without emancipating human thought from the ideological barriers erected by exploiting classes. And this means the end of all forms of idealism and of static and metaphysical thinking. The bourgeoisie can use any kind of pragmatic justification of expediency, but the working class requires a positive scientific approach to the world, society, history, and the laws of social movement.

The theoretical problems of the future involved in mankind's ever expanding knowledge of natural and social laws and ever developing use of them to solve its problems, will be infinitely greater in number and scope than ever before. But they will be problems arising in specific fields or from inter-relations of different specific fields and will be dealt with and resolved by experts in these fields, not by people trained in historical philosophy. Or they will be such methodological problems as fall into the fields of logic and dialectics which, Engels believed, would be all that remain of historic philosophy. Finally, the study of the history of philosophy will occupy a prominent place. It will do so, however, not in virtue of the problems it will help men to solve, but because of the immense light it will shed on man's historic struggles to understand and master his world.

The logic of the Marxist position is indisputable and is implied by Engels' statement that the great basic question of all philosophy has been that of the relation of thinking to being, the subject of Chapter III. That question is now completely resolvable at the present level of scientific development. It is not resolved, however, only because of present social relations based on the private ownership of the instruments of production. The theoretical conditions for the elimination or solution of the traditional questions of philosophy are at hand. The practical conditions are as follows:

(1) The achievement of a classless society and with it the elimination of all classes interested in and capable of maintaining superstition, of believing and teaching anything but a scientific approach to nature and man. Such thinkers as Epicurus, Bacon and Diderot dreamed of such a state of affairs, but in exploitative society it could be only a dream. Now, however, the path to its realization is clearly represented by the aims of socialism and communism.

(2) The second condition for the actual "withering away"

of philosophy is the education of all people in a scientific approach to the questions of nature, life, and society. This, of course, is the necessary consequent of the first condition and is dependent on it. The current direction of the imperialist bourgeoisie in this respect is shown graphically in the recent addition by the Congress of the United States of the phrase "under God" to the oath of allegiance to be sworn to the flag by school children and members of the armed forces, as well as by adding "In God We Trust" to postage stamps. Why that becomes necessary 178 years after the founding of our Republic can be explained only by the growing intensity of the struggle between the forces of progress and reaction on a world scale.

But all people can be brought up to approach the world solely in scientific terms and they will be when the dominant forces in society wish it, as in the countries of socialism today. And when all people ask from childhood such questions as "What is the world made of?" "What makes the sun hot?" and the like, instead of "Who made the world?" or "Who made the sun hot?" philosophy, as we have known it, will be replaced by science.

(3) But a third condition, requisite for the fulfillment of the second is the unification, in practical daily life, of science, technology and social relations so that there are no mysterious cataclysms, no forces unknowable and incapable of human control, but only things we do not yet know but are on the way of finding out.

Through this process of social transformation, philosophy in its traditional form will come to an end. It will do so not because it was useless but because it will have achieved its true goal. All mankind will have moved from mythology to science in every realm of thought and action. Only the achievement of socialism and the complete elimination of conflicting economic classes can bring mankind to this goal. That alone can bring the end of exploiting society, and with it the end of all superstition, of all vestiges of man's primitive ignorance. This transition constitutes indeed a veritable revolution in human thought, a revolution which can come about only through a revolution in human society. It is a necessary concomitant, an inevitable feature of mankind's final struggle against oppression and all forms of the exploitation of man by man.

Today hundreds of millions of people are freeing themselves from one or another form of bondage and are building to overcome poverty forever. Oppressed classes have rebelled before, but all previous social revolutions, while marking an historical advance, have established only a new form of exploitation and have replaced one kind of superstition by another. Thomas Hobbes once defined the difference between religion and superstition solely in terms of social acceptability. We call, he said, "fear of powers invisible" derived from tales or legends not socially acceptable "superstition." But if the tales are conventionally approved, we call it "religion." But respectability is relative, and while one section of society is satisfied with religion, sections of the intellectuals require philosophical idealism and those who attempt to be ultra "modern" require and use positivism and pragmatism. It is not too much to say that some of the philosophy taught in our colleges and universities is a respectable form of superstition and has as little of a future as the class whose philosophy it is.

Meanwhile the official spokesmen of the ruling class are making a mighty effort to keep religion as a mainstay of its shaky rule. Government and big business join in this effort and neither politicians, generals, nor corporation presidents can speak of preparation for war on the socialist world without a pious invocation to the deity. They sound as holy as any leaders of the medieval crusades against the "infidel Moslem." General Omar Bradley has solemnly proclaimed: "Our knowledge of science has clearly outstripped our capacity to control it. We have too many men of science; too few men of God. We have grasped the mystery of the atom and rejected the Sermon on the Mount. . . . Ours is a world of nuclear giants and ethical infants."

The struggle being waged today by great masses of workers and peasants, inseparably linked with the national and colonial liberation struggles against imperialism, is the beginning of the movement of all mankind into a scientific materialist world outlook. It is the coming of age of the human species—the beginning of the achievement of that stature which enables the masses of men and women to say for the first time: "We need no blinders, we need no reservations. Only truth has freed us and can help us keep our freedom."

It is not an accident but an inevitable historic process that

Chinese workers, peasants, students, are today studying dialectical and historical materialism. This gives them what no Confucianism, no Buddhism, no Christianity, no "Western" bourgeois philosophy could possibly give. Together with the study of economics and natural science it becomes their meat and drink, their way of organizing their world, their way of controlling nature collectively. All the other ideologies could offer them only ways of controlling or of being controlled by their fellows. Countless millions of dollars and the efforts of innumerable devoted missionaries could bring Christianity or "Western philosophy" to only a handful of Chinese. But the people's own struggles for millet and rice, national independence and industrialization, guided by the theory formulated by the great working class teachers and leaders of the world, are bringing them in a few brief years across centuries to a scientific materialist world view.

The bold and fearless materialism of Democritus, Epicurus and Lucretius waited unattended outside the stronghold of ancient slave power. The time was not ripe for a scientific outlook that could move the masses to storm and capture the citadels of power themselves. But today, thanks to the rise of capitalism and the physical and intellectual forces it has unleashed on the part of its "grave diggers," the working class, the "slaves" have a philosophy of their own. This is not one that consoles them, not one that removes the artificial flowers that decorate the chains that bind them, but one which, in Marx's famous phrase, enables them to throw off the chains that they may enjoy the living flowers.

One need only think of the horrible sufferings of the enslaved builders of the Egyptian pyramids, of the miserable slaves or starving "proletarians" of Rome, of the serfs of medieval Europe, of the peasants driven from the land for the sheep enclosures in England, or the Negro slaves of the United States, to realize that it was always done through the combination of the whip and the knout with the medicine-man and the priest. Now, for the first time, the very descendants of those who survived the famine and pestilence of the ancient and modern poor, are moving from superstition to science. They may now be devout Catholics as in Italy, or Moslems as in Indonesia, but the very process of their struggles against oppression and exploitation for peace and decent living standards, is at the same time the process of liberation from mythology, from the spiritual exploitation of the modern descendants of the medicine-men.

Thus through the great mass struggles of the twentieth century for national freedom, for peace, democracy and, ultimately, socialism, the age-old dream of the materialists of a mankind guided by science in the solution of all its problems is becoming a reality. The superstition that is the ideological expression of ignorance and exploitation cannot survive a classless society. Bourgeois philosophy has reached a dead-end. The rise of Marxism as the philosophy of the working class heralds a new age. The triumph of socialism in one-third of the earth and in the minds of millions of oppressed peoples everywhere, led by the teachings of Marx, Lenin and other great progressive teachers of mankind is bringing the new age to birth. And as Marx and Engels liked to refer to this movement as that from the prehistoric age of man to the historic, so can we also call it mankind's movement from a pre-scientific to a scientific world outlook.

CHAPTER II

A NEW WORLD OUTLOOK

CAPITALISM GAVE rise to the new class of wage workers who were driven by want into the cities, deprived of everything but their labor power. But this new proletariat was destined to be the creator of a new world order. It was destined to revolutionize the whole time-honored way in which people had thought about their world. It knew no political economy, but was to transform it into a science of social planning. It knew no philosophy, but was to convert it from the speculative interpretation of the world to a science of changing it. In "realizing" philosophy, to use Marx's expression, it was to liberate itself. In liberating itself it was to revolutionize philosophy.

Out of the primitive superstition, magic and mythology of early communal society—a magic designed primarily for man's control over the forces of nature outside him—came the world's religions. These, however, were not designed as was magic, for the administering of things, but for the administering of people. This was a basic requirement of class society.

But now a new class arises, a product of the revolution in production that capitalism had brought about. This class is forced by the conditions of its life to arm itself with the science that had developed, to create a new scientific materialist world view—a view designed for the organizing of people to the end of their mastery over things. And as this class, under communism, will bring an end to the state as the classic form of administration over men and substitute for it the administration by men over things, so too does it put an end to all modes and forms of thought that subordinate people to people—producers to owners, women to men, manual workers to intellectual workers, the darker peoples of the earth to the whites. It will do this to the end that mankind as a whole may devote all its energies to the

29

collective mastery of nature for humanity's sake. This is the true humanism, and the bearer of it is the working class.

Why is it that this class can accomplish such world-historical ends? Why it, rather than the favored patrician slave-owners of the ancient world? Why the working class rather than the nobles and grandees of the ages of feudalism, East and West? Why it, rather than the owners of industry able to hire the best brains of society as their thinkers, their apologists? Why the working class—exploited and oppressed in mines and factories, the dispossessed class that has nothing to sell but its hands?

Here lay the great wisdom of Marx and Engels. Contrary to the Utopian Socialists of the early nineteenth century who saw in the working class only the most suffering class, they saw in it the class which held the key to the future. Their most basic insight, that which launched Marxism into the world, was that the workers in modern capitalist industry constituted that force precisely which "had nothing to lose but its chains," and "a world to win." That they must inevitably struggle and learn, learn and struggle, from minor victories to greater victories, from temporary defeats to that greatest victory of all—the reconstruction of society on socialist lines.

Three features of the position of the working class determine the form and content of its thought and enable it to revolutionize philosophy. The first concerns its relation to nature. It is the first producing class in world history to have its own world view. It enters into entirely different relations with nature than does any other class in our society or any class that previously contributed to philosophy. It is the class that does the work of the world. Its relations to nature are not those of the ancient Greek slave-owner, the feudal lord or the feudal monk, or the bourgeois scholar and academician. Their relations to nature are of a speculative kind. To borrow a pointed expression of Marx's, they *stand* in relation to nature, but the working class is engaged in *active* relations, producing the food, clothing, and shelter required for the maintenance of life. Nature, things, are not there to be contemplated or speculated about, they are there to be worked up into articles of consumption. Matter is not an abstract category but the name for the raw materials which labor works up, the tools that must be employed, the finished products, as well as the laborer and the labor process itself. This different relationship to nature from that of all previous classes and their philosophies, gives working class thought a radically different starting point and direction in respect to nature and to knowledge.

The second characteristic feature of the working class that determines its thought is its need for truth and nothing but the truth. All classes struggling for power need a certain amount of truth. Indeed, any class in power requires some truth just to keep its power another day. But the degrees vary immensely. In all exploiting society a great amount of falsehood in the form of mythology is required. The work by Professor Barrows Dunham, *Man Against Myth*, exhibits in rich detail the myths required to keep the existing capitalist order going another day. What is not revealed in Dunham's book is that it is not *man* in the abstract, but the working class that is against myth and that must destroy all mythology. The late Robert Briffault remarked somewhere that "the price of ignorance is eternal vigilance." He meant that it takes immense effort, an enormous apparatus and constant care for the ruling classes to keep the masses ignorant, to keep them constantly doped with superstition. It does not just happen; it does not take care of itself. One needs only to think of the billions, literally, spent in the United States each year to drug the public with anti-materialist propaganda, with white chauvinism, male supremacy, "people's capitalism," the Horatio Alger myths, and so on.

But one might ask if workers are not as subject to such propaganda and as gullible as members of other classes. Are not the workers of our country as filled with such mythology as any group or class in industrialized countries? To ask that question is to miss the whole point. It is precisely the historical necessity, the inevitable destiny of the working class to overcome this mythology and superstition by liberating society from the forces and conditions that have created and perpetuated it.

The modern industrial working class needs the truth and nothing but the truth because falsehood and illusion will only hinder it in the accomplishment of its task—its own emancipation and the liberation of all mankind from exploitation, oppression and war. It needs no divine blessing on things as they are. It needs no illusions about its conditions. It is the first class in world history that can view nature as it finds without reservations, without subtractions or fanciful additions. The real interests of the working class run counter to religion. It is less interested in interpreting nature than in mastering it for human purposes.

The novelist, Charles Kingsley, a Canon of the Church of England, described beautifully in 1848 the way the bourgeoisie has employed religion to serve its class interests: "We have used the Bible as if it were the special constable's handbook,—*an opium dose for keeping beasts of burden patient while they were being overloaded,*—a mere book to keep the poor in order."¹ The worker plainly needs not the "opium dose" but rather needs to cease being a beast of burden.

The rising bourgeoisie needed physical science. It needed social science, too, and made enormous advances in two main areas. It sought to make a science of politics, and from Machiavelli, Grotius and Puffendorf to Harrington, Locke, Madison and Hamilton, it achieved notable results in the direction of a realistic understanding of social forces and the nature of state power. In the field of political economy it began virtually where Aristotle left off and ended in Adam Smith and Ricardo with most of the essentials of a science of social production and distribution. It required these social sciences up to that point when its contradictions began to appear in the vivid form of economic crises and when the working class began to challenge its rule in the second quarter of the nineteenth century.

Karl Marx, in his preface to the second edition of the first volume of *Capital* in 1873, expressed this drastic retreat of bourgeois social thought as follows:

> Thenceforth, the class-struggle, practically as well as theoretically, took on more and more outspoken and threatening forms. It sounded the knell of scientific bourgeois economy. It was thenceforth no longer a question, whether this theorem or that was true, but whether it was useful to capital or harmful, expedient or inexpedient, politically dangerous or not. In place of disinterested enquirers, there were hired prize-fighters; in place of genuine scientific research, the bad conscience and the evil intent of apologetics.²

Since that time the bourgeoisie has had to substitute mythology for genuine social science, subjective idealism for a materialist approach to politics and economics, and has sought in pragmatism even to raise "expediency" to the high level of philosophical principle, as when William James defined *"The True"* as *"only the expedient in the way of our thinking."*³ But while the bourgeoisie has been forced by its position to renounce and forsake the social science it had achieved, nothing, now or in the future, can keep the working class and collective mankind, from seeking truth in every sphere by the methods of the sciences.

The third distinctive feature of the position of the working class in world history is that it need put no limits to change. Any exploiting class is committed by its position to the maintenance of existing relations of production, or in other words, to existing class relations, to the *status quo*. Any class struggling for power in order to be a new exploiting class seeks change only up to a certain point—the consolidation of its power. After that it abhors change. It celebrates the revolution by which it got to power while using every waking moment and all its energy to ensure that there will be no more revolutions. But the working class envisions endless change. It can do always what the bourgeoisie dared do only in scattered brief moments—in the England of Bacon to Locke, in the France of the Encyclopedists and Condorcet, and in the England and the United States of Godwin, Paine and Jefferson.

The working class is the first class in world history that can conceive of, and devote itself to, unending change and progress. This is the reason it is the first class in history that can develop a fully dialectical world view and the science of dialectics itself. It can do this not only because it envisages endless development and the infinite perfectability of mankind, but also because it is forced to recognize the role of struggle, conflict, and contradiction in all development. Hegel, representing the young, weak, and timid German bourgeoisie, inspired by the achievements of the "industrial revolution" in England and the great French Revolution, made an immense contribution to dialectics. He resuscitated the brilliant insights of the ancient Heracleitus, but his class position forced him to confine them in a "system" that was tightly closed. Marx and Engels, knowing Hegel's philosophy most intimately, were able to liberate dialectics from its bourgeois prison house only through their direct experience with, and participation in, the struggles of the industrial proletariat of England, France, and Germany. If they gave dialectics to the working class movement it was only because this movement required and was able to use and develop dialectics.

Such are the distinctive features of working class thought,

the reflection in consciousness of the actual class conflict. That it was not workers themselves who first developed dialectical and historical materialism, illustrates only the virtual impossibility of industrial workers of the second quarter of the nineteenth century acquiring advanced education in philosophy and the sciences. One, indeed, Joseph Dietzgen, the German tanner, did something of this himself. But Marxism, dialectical material- ism, a fully scientific approach to nature, society, and history, required the combination of working class experience in modern capitalist production and of training in the best thought of pre- vious classes. It is not an accident that it came from Germans, because of the peculiar position of the then very young Ger- man bourgeoisie and its need to struggle against a long outlived feudalism. It is also no accident that it came from Germans who got into active participation in the more advanced class struggle in England and France. Socialism and Communism were in the very air that the young Marx and Engels breathed when they left their homeland. They did not discover or invent it. They were especially equipped to give it scientific formulation, to convert it, as the famous phrase runs, from a dream into a reality, from utopianism to science. Through their immense theoretical background and their experiences in the struggles of the workers they both revolutionized philosophy and forged a new revolutionary theory for the working class.

The form of working class thought is scientific. This means that there is no specific philosophical form or system as with almost all previous philosophy. As there is no system of philos- ophy over and above the sciences, so there is no special form of philosophy. This fact bothers the academicians no end. They like philosophical systems where things are nicely fitted together and well lubricated, as Professor B. A. G. Fuller has said, "so that either what looks good seems true, or what seems true looks good."[4]

The academic philosophers claim they cannot find Marxist philosophy. As one distinguished professor once told me, he has been unable to find Lenin's "metaphysics." The answer is, simply, that Lenin had no metaphysics. Neither Marx nor Engels wrote any book on *philosophy* in the sense of the *systems* of the classic tradition. But every book they wrote was permeated by a philos- ophy of a new kind. This consists of a materialist interpretation or conception of all the phenomena of nature and society, and of a dialectical approach to their movement. But this is nothing else than the world as the sciences and the whole body of human experience reveal it to us. It is "nature without reservations," it is the world without illusions, a position possible only to a class which seeks the abolition of all classes.

If the form of this philosophy is thus indefinite how can its content be defined? This, too, is difficult because as can be seen from the above, Marxist philosophy has no special content, over and above the sciences, with the exception of dialectics and its laws. The exception is itself most significant. It means that instead of possessing an over-all, complete world system, Marxist philosophy's only special content, outside of its fight for a scientific materialist approach to all questions, is the most generalized form of the laws of motion of thought and of things. Every science, to be science at all, must deal with the laws of motion, of development, of its own subject matter.

All that has been left for philosophy as a special subject matter apart from all others is the study and analysis of these laws, generalizing from the various sciences to find the most basic and universal forms that motion and development take. The difference from traditional philosophy, in short, is that instead of trying to form an ultimate system of the world, Marxist materialism forever explores and analyses the laws of motion of all phenomena of nature, society, and thought. By doing this it becomes a guide to scientists in all specialized fields.

The above statement is not to be confused with the idea that Marxism has no body of doctrine but is only a method. When Engels said, "Our theory is not a dogma, but a guide to action," he did not mean that Marxist political economy and the materialist interpretation of history were not developed bodies of principles, sciences of the real world. He was not a pragmatist who teaches that we are always about to learn, but never have learned. He was merely emphasizing a basic feature of all Marxist thought, namely, that it does not claim to possess finality for all times, places, and circumstances. Lenin expressed this idea very clearly in a sentence in his *Materialism and Empirio-Criticism*: "The sole conclusion to be drawn from the opinion of the Marxists that Marx's theory is an objective truth is that by following the *path* of Marxian theory we shall draw closer and closer to objective truth (without ever exhausting it); but by following *any other path* we shall arrive at nothing but confusion and lies."[5]

The same proposition holds true for Marxist philosophy. Hundreds of thousands of years of human life and thousands of years of civilization with its development of science and technology enable us to assert—once the barriers erected by exploiting classes are removed—certain things about the world, about ourselves and our relations to the nature outside us, about our knowledge and social relations. It is these propositions, including the laws of dialectics, which constitute the heart of Marxist philosophy, of dialectical and historical materialism. Some of them will be developed at length in the succeeding chapters.

It is desirable, first, to get the over-all approach that characterizes this philosophy as that of the revolutionary working class. This approach constitutes the core of historical materialism, and is Marx's greatest and most distinctive contribution. Practically, it stands at the center of scientific socialist principles: first, that production is the material foundation of human life, and second, that the relations of production constitute the base on which the whole ideological superstructure of society rests.

The material basis of human life lies in production, in labor. In one of Plato's dialogues man is defined as a featherless biped. He is that, to be sure, but it is scarcely the most significant thing about him. For Aristotle he was a rational animal. He is that, too, but the statement tells little about how he got that way and the nature and direction of his development. For Marx and Engels labor is the key to man's nature and his individual and social development. He is the animal who produces his means of subsistence and in doing so makes his own nature and his social world. To all exploiting classes, labor was the curse it was represented to be in the Bible when, as a result of Adam's sin, he was told that henceforth: "In the sweat of thy face shalt thou eat bread." But that is precisely the way he and his ancestors had always been earning their bread. The very phrase suggests the transition from communal to class society. For in the latter, labor is a curse pronounced on the majority for the benefit of the few.

A classic expression of this attitude towards manual labor

was given in a purported statement of Socrates, quoted by Xenophon.

What are rightly called the mechanical arts carry a social stigma and are rightly dishonored in our cities. For these arts damage the bodies of those who work at them or who have charge of them, by compelling the workers to a sedentary life and to an indoor life, by compelling them indeed, in some cases to spend the whole day by the fire. This physical degeneration results also in deterioration of the soul. Furthermore, the workers at these trades simply have not got the time to perform the offices of friendship or of citizenship. Consequently they are looked upon as bad friends and bad patriots. And in some cities, especially the warlike ones, it is not legal for a citizen to ply a mechanical trade.[6]

In similar vein Plato refers to an oracle which says that the city shall perish when it is guarded by workers and farmers.[7] And Aristotle adds that "manual workers are like certain lifeless things which act indeed, but act without knowing what they do."[8] So has labor always been regarded in class society, for the simple reason that its performance or non-performance is the simplest and most obvious distinction between exploiters and exploited, between those who regard themselves as the better people and those who do the work of the world.

How, then, could any but a laboring class ever recognize the simple truth that it is labor, essentially, that distinguishes man from the lower animals, labor that has shaped his nature, and labor which gives the human race the power of determining its destiny? It was left therefore to the spokesmen of the modern industrial proletariat to say: "Men can be distinguished from animals by consciousness, by religion or anything else you like. They themselves begin to distinguish themselves from animals as soon as they begin to *produce* their means of subsistence, a step which is conditioned by their physical organization. By producing their means of subsistence men are indirectly producing their actual material life."[9]

Frederick Engels wrote many years later that labor "is the primary basic condition for all human existence, and this to such an extent that, in a sense, we have to say that labor created man himself."[10] Anyone can notice the direct connection between this proposition and the doctrine that the development of the human hand preceded, made possible and expedited the development of the human brain and intelligence. This very controversy, which goes back to Anaxagoras and Aristotle, beautifully illustrates the second principle to be discussed, namely that the relations of production determine the whole ideological superstructure.

Pre-Marxist materialists sought the material base of man and society in everything but the production process. They found it in food, and then proceeded to deduce national differences from different eating habits. Or they found it in climate and geography, or solely in man's physical structure as something static which just happened to come about. They looked on this earth, at least, and not in some other realm like the idealists, but they did not look in the right place. Only dialectical materialists, only theoretical representatives of the working class could see, as Marx and Engels saw, that the process whereby men produce their means of subsistence is at the same time the process that shapes the nature of man himself. They alone saw that producing our food, clothing, and shelter did something to us—something that can be seen only when the barriers have been torn down between mind and matter, physical and intellectual labor, material well being and a so-called "higher" or spiritual life. They wrote:

> This mode of production must not be considered simply as being the reproduction of the physical existence of the individuals. Rather it is a definite form of activity of these individuals, a definite form of expressing their life, a definite *mode of life* on their part. As individuals express their life, so they are. What they are, therefore, coincides with their production, both with *what* they produce and with *how* they produce. The nature of individuals thus depends on the material conditions determining their production.[11]

As will be shown in the final chapter, this discovery lays the basis for the only valid conception of human freedom. It puts the finger on exactly that which mankind can learn to master, and through mastering control the conditions of his life—the labor process, the process of production. All previous theories attempted to "elevate" man by glorifying his intellect, by *freeing* him from the domination of the material. This theory does full justice to human nature by showing precisely in what man's distinction from the animals consists. Here, as in so many things, the *idealist* theory covered up brutal material conditions, while the materialist theory reveals the true meaning and direction of human *ideals*. The animal does not produce, it merely finds the means of its subsistence. Man makes them and in doing so is constantly making and re-making himself. His goal must be to produce his means of subsistence ever more adequately and in ways worthy of his nature, and its potentialities.

The second basic Marxist principle is this: how people produce—what they produce, what they produce it with, and the relations to one another in the process—conditions all the rest of their life and thought. This is expressed with exemplary directness and simplicity in Stalin's *Dialectical and Historical Materialism*. There the question is asked: "What . . . is the chief force in the complex of conditions of material life of society which determines the physiognomy of society, the character of the social system, the development of society from one system to another?" What, in other words, is the material basis of society? The answer is:

This force, historical materialism holds, is the *method of procuring the means* of life necessary for human existence, the *mode of production of material values*—food, clothing, footwear, houses, fuel, instruments of production, etc.—which are indispensable for the life and development of society. . . .

The *instruments of production* wherewith the material values are produced, the *people* who operate the instruments of production and carry on the production of material values thanks to a certain *production experience* and *labor skill*—all these elements jointly constitute the *production forces* of society. . . .

Another aspect of production, another aspect of the mode of production, is the relation of men to each other in the process of production, men's *relations of production*. Men carry on a struggle against nature and utilize nature for the production of material values not in isolation from each other, not as separate individuals, but in common, in groups, in societies. Production, therefore, is at all times and under all conditions *social* production. In the production of material values men enter into mutual relations of one kind or another within production, into relations of production of one kind or another. These may be relations of cooperation and mutual help between people who are free from exploitation; they may be relations of domination and subordination; and, lastly, they may be transitional from one form of relations of production to another. But whatever the character of the relations of production may be, always and in every system, they constitute just as essential an element of production as the productive forces of society.[12]

A number of important things are to be noticed here. One is that production is social, not individual. It is not carried on

by an Adam alone in a Garden of Eden, nor, in its special bourgeois form, by a Robinson Crusoe on a desert island. It is
carried on by people in the closest interdependence and inter-
relation.

Another special feature of the Marxist approach is the emphasis on the instruments or tools of production. People do not
just produce, but do so in particular ways with particular tools,
instruments, or machines. These are provided by their prede-
cessors, for any given generation, but if people are to use them
they must also be capable of producing and reproducing them.
And with any given tools go a whole set of skills acquired in
the process of developing the tools. As people make the tools
it could also be said that the tools make the people. Do we
produce our food with wooden sticks to scratch the soil or with
tractors pulling great steel ploughs? As we produce, so are we.

One of the most extraordinary limitations of all pre-Marxist
philosophy was the lack of attention given to the instruments
of production. Aristotle, for example, was so preoccupied with
the invention of those arts which "did not aim at utility" that he
assumed the useful ones (those required for production) were
already fully developed. He further says that the inventors of
the non-useful arts and techniques "were naturally always regarded as wiser than the inventors of the former."[13]

Another significant feature of the Marxist position is its emphasis on the "production experience and *labor skill*" of the
workers who use the instruments available at any given time.
To all classical thinkers such virtues belonged solely to the
class which owned the instruments. They gave themselves the
credit for the skill involved in their use. Nothing, however, better proves this Marxist point than does modern industry. Modern warfare reflects it with perfect directness. When free public
compulsory education was established it was because literacy,
elementary mathematics, and so forth had become increasingly
necessary for workers to use the new instruments of production
that had been developed.

Again, the passage is pointing out that there are not only
tools of production, but *relations* into which people enter with
one another in order to use them. A certain role is ascribed
to the instruments, even by many bourgeois thinkers, especially
those with mechanical materialist tendencies. They, indeed,

often make them the sole and distinct driving force of history.[14] This is a convenient way of appearing to be materialist in social theory while still being perfectly safe. For if the relations of production are disregarded and all social change is traceable directly to changes in the instruments or tools of production, the role of classes and the class struggle is completely ignored. This is one of the most important and most frequently confused points in Marxist historical materialism. It is not a question of economic "factors" or of non-economic factors, but simply that the material foundation of society is the mode of production, and this consists of two interdependent parts, the forces and the relations of production. Of these two, it is changes in the forces of production, in the first instance, which determine the character of, and changes in, the relations of production. And it is the relations of production that constitute the base on which the whole institutional and ideological superstructure rests. By-passing the relations of production is to by-pass the most fundamental of all human relations, those on which all others are built. The instruments, in short, are not of themselves the determining force of any given form of society or of the direction of its development, but they operate solely through the relations of people involved in their use—through the relations of those who own them to those who actually use them in production.

Classes and class struggle were known prior to Marxism, but not the concept of *relations of production*. The simple reason for this is one aspect of what Marx called the fetishism of commodities, the commodities being, in this case, the capital goods required for all production. They were considered only as things, and people were conceived as entering into relations with these things. Thus ownership of mules or tractors was mistakenly thought of as the relation of people to these things, instead of to one another. It was Marxism that first pointed out that the relations of ownership and non-ownership were relations only of people to one another, and these ownership relations "constitute just as essential an element of production as the productive forces of society."

Such is the material base of society. But one might ask what this has to do with philosophy. The classic philosophers never dealt with such questions and their disciples do not to this day.

Classic philosophy, in ignoring the role of labor, similarly and necessarily ignored the role of the productive forces and the relations of production. The meaning and consequence of ignoring productive forces has already been explained. The ignoring of production relations has still more direct effects on philosophy. To ignore the role of labor is to take an idealist rather than a materialist outlook on the universe and on society. It is to put mind before matter, thinking before being. To ignore the mode of production as the determinant of the physiognomy, the character of a society, is to fail utterly to provide any possible foundation for the origin of ideas in human history, the origin of customs and traditions, political and religious systems, religion, ethics, philosophy, aesthetics, and all the other aspects of the superstructure.

Marx and Engels in their middle twenties wrote of the Young Hegelians of their day: "It has not occurred to any one of these philosophers to inquire into the connection of German philosophy with German reality, the relation of their criticism to their own material surroundings."[15] It had never occurred to *any* philosophers to do this—to inquire into the connection of their thought with their reality, with their material surroundings, the mode of production and its class relations. It still does not occur to the academicians. This idea was a new revolutionary insight, possible only to the modern working-class movement. Other classes live and have lived in a topsy-turvy world, in which material surroundings are considered the effect of their ideas, while their ideas are simply self-productions of their own consciousness. This doctrine of historical materialism introduces partisanship into philosophy, and, indeed, all forms of ideology, not by putting it there but by showing that it is inescapable.

Now that the material base of society has been uncovered, some further considerations of the superstructure built upon it are in order. It was Hegel who first saw that the philosophy of a time was "contemporaneous with a particular constitution of the people amongst whom it makes its appearance. . . ." But then Hegel asks the final question: Which comes first, what caused what? And after his extraordinary achievement in seeing something of the inter-relation of the various elements of the superstructure with one another, Hegel blithely answered: "po-

litical history, forms of government, art and religion are not related to philosophy as its causes, nor, on the other hand, is philosophy the ground of their existence—one and all have the same common root, the spirit of the time."[16]
What Hegel could not see, Marx saw. And he tells us:

In the social production which men carry on they enter into definite relations that are indispensable and independent of their will; these relations of production correspond to a definite stage of development of their material powers of production. The sum total of these relations of production constitutes the economic structure of society—the real foundation, on which rise legal and political superstructures and to which correspond definite forms of social consciousness. The mode of production in material life determines the general character of the social, political and spiritual processes of life. It is not the consciousness of men that determines their existence, but, on the contrary, their social existence determines their consciousness.[17]

Thus, in this way, the young Marx, about 1845, solved the problem that had not even been raised prior to Hegel, and which Hegel could not solve. His discovery in no way belittles ideas and their role, consciousness and its forms. Indeed, by correctly placing them in the historical process, it extricates them for the first time from the pitfall of the metaphysical approach, namely that ideas were *mere* ideas. Now it is clear that ideas not only have roots in the material conditions of life but are significant precisely to the extent that they can react upon these roots and change them.

No longer can ideas appear to come from disembodied minds. No longer can music appear to be divorced from ideology generally, and ideology from the relations of production. No longer can anyone argue before the bar of working-class thought that he has an idea, paints a picture, writes a symphony, interprets the law, makes a moral judgment, or performs a scientific experiment, in complete independence of the kind of society he or she lives in, or the class which holds his allegiance. As Marx and Engels put it:

Morality, religion, metaphysics, all the rest of ideology and their corresponding forms of consciousness, thus no longer retain the semblance of independence. They have no history, no development; but men, developing their material production and their material intercourse, alter, along with this their real existence, their thinking and the products of their thinking. Life is not determined by consciousness, but consciousness by life.[18]

Such an analysis of the relation of consciousness and thought to social reality can be only anathema to those whose life is devoted to maintaining the illusion that ideas are "pure," totally independent of a given society or class. For them to accept this Marxist view is to deny the validity of their whole outlook. They would be required either to admit they live a lie, which is to commit intellectual suicide, or to change their class allegiance and with it their whole mode of life and thought.

But the more advanced apologists for a dying order do not give up this easily. They have two shots yet to fire. The first is that Marxists then, too, are partisan, as partisan as they claim the bourgeois thinkers are, or else they contradict themselves. This charge has been leveled in innumerable books and articles. The second charge is that Marxists, through their confession of partisanship, have renounced truth for the class struggle.

The two objections are really one: that truth and partisanship are incompatible and mutually destructive. And there is one answer. Marxists are partisan: they have never denied it. They neither need nor want to deny it. The others are partisan too, but they dare not admit it. This is one of the salient facts of the intellectual world of the twentieth century. The partisans of the bourgeoisie today, unlike their forebears of the seventeenth and eighteenth centuries, dare not confess their partisanship. To do so is to confess intellectual bankruptcy because capitalism is theoretically bankrupt. They take refuge, therefore, in claims to pure objectivity and impartiality. They defend imperialism out of the demands of "pure reason," "freedom" and the "dignity of the individual," not because they are aligned with the bourgeoisie and identify their interests with it.

When Marx set forth the principle that all forms of ideology express class relations and reflect partiality to one class or another, he understood perfectly well that this held for him, too. Marxism, in fact, is accused both of intense partisanship and moral bias on one hand, and of its opposite, pure objective science that disregards all moral values on the other. The answer to this apparent dilemma of the relationship of partisanship and truth is so simple that it need only be stated to be understood by anyone not blinded by bourgeois partisanship.

First, it must be established at the outset that Marxists believe there is truth, objective truth. Indeed, while bourgeois philosophy has largely given up the very concept of truth (Dewey substitutes "warranted assertibility"), Marxism upholds it as the reflection in our minds of the objective reality outside. Second, there is no necessary antagonism between partisanship and truth. The search for truth, like all other human quests and endeavors, must be motivated. And there is no innate motive in human beings to seek truth. Certain reactionary bourgeois philosophers, indeed, such as Nietzsche, have made dissimulation the prime function of intelligence. Who would dare say that Plato's or John Dewey's primary concern was truth? And who could deny that the Ionians, the early modern materialists, really wanted truth? A progressive class, one that can carry forward the development of the forces of production, requires truth and ever more of it. It needs truth for the extension of its power and for greater mastery over nature. A reactionary class fears truth because truth threatens its maintenance of power. It takes refuge in falsehood and mythology.

Thus the question is not the abstract one of partisanship versus truth, but partisanship to what? The need of the working class for truth, and nothing but truth, has already been discussed. The need of the bourgeoisie, especially in the epoch of imperialism, for falsehood, has likewise been dealt with. The conclusion is that the highest possible guarantee of the truth of Marxism is its intense partisanship to the working class and its struggle for liberation. Marxists are proud of their partisanship because it places them in the vanguard of the struggle for human freedom and the advancement of human knowledge.

Historical materialism has immense implications for economic and political thought and action. But our problem here is confined to its impact on philosophy and ideology generally. It provides the explanation for the working class revolution in philosophy. It alone explains why and how this class could transform the previous structure of mankind's theoretical world. It explains why bourgeois thought today is dead, as the thought of a class with no future. It explains why falsehood and superstition—from racism to extra-sensory perception, from moral rearmament to the imperialist myth of "the Free World"—exist side by side with such an epoch-making scientific discovery as

the utilization of atomic energy. Historical materialism is hated
by the bourgeois apologists because it tells its followers not
to take, on its face value, any idea advanced by those who make
their living as ideologists in official capitalist society, whether
in the sciences, the arts, or philosophy. Marx could certainly
have said of historical materialism what he wrote of materialist dialectics, for it is the application of this very materialist
dialectics to society:

> It is a scandal and abomination to bourgeoisdom and its doctrinaire
> professors, because it includes in its comprehension an affirmative recog-
> nition of the existing state of things, at the same time also, the recogni-
> tion of the negation of that state, of its inevitable breaking up; because
> it regards every historically developed social form as in fluid movement,
> and therefore takes into account its transient nature not less than its mo-
> mentary existence; because it lets nothing impose upon it, and is, in its
> essence, critical and revolutionary.[19]

As the principles of dialectical materialism provide the theoretical foundation for historical materialism, so does this historical materialism provide the social and historical foundation and
explanation for the rise and content of dialectical materialism.
In reality, they are two aspects of one and the same world outlook, separable only for convenience. Neither aspect, nor the two
in their mutual interdependence, constitutes a philosophy in the
old sense. They are simply the broadest generalizations concerning nature, society, and the laws of their development, mankind at this stage of its history is entitled to make. They are
the product of all social experience, science, technology, and
industry. They provide the indispensable basis for any science,
natural or social. They do not constitute a philosophy in the old
sense of a metaphysics, standing over and above the sciences.
Marx and Engels expressed this most forcefully in *The German
Ideology*: "Actually, when we conceive things thus, as they really
are and happened, every profound philosophical problem is resolved . . . quite simply into an empirical fact."[20]

Even such a statement would be made into a mountain of
insoluble problems by contemporary bourgeois philosophers.
The positivists, for example, could do this because they interpret empirical facts not as the concrete experience of people,
but as some kind of process of sensation in a disembodied "mind."

They deny, for example, that the existence of anything outside of our minds is an empirical fact. These questions will be taken up in some detail in the chapter on knowledge. The point here is that certain principles, derived from the whole of human experience, are necessary if we are to approach our world scientifically, while the development of science has confirmed and continues to reinforce these principles.

But what are these principles that put an end to the old philosophy, that revolutionize philosophy, that provide the foundation for both a new world outlook and a new world? The most basic principles of Marxist scientific materialism may be summarized as follows:

This materialism holds that there is an objective world, existing independent of human consciousness. It existed, in fact, prior to any life and consciousness. We are 'born into a world we did not make and it remains after our or any other thought and personality cease to exist.

It believes that this objective reality is material, not mental or spiritual. This means simply that it consists of matter, not mind, and operates in accordance with the laws of motion of matter, and not in accordance with purposes, aims, or other characteristics of beings equipped with "mind" or consciousness.

In contrast to pre-Marxist materialism, Marxism holds that the world consists of events and processes in complex interrelation and interaction, where nothing exists in isolation and nothing stands still. All nature is in constant change and development through its own inherent contradictions, and growth and change take place not merely gradually but by leaps from one qualitative level to another.

From the view that matter is primary it necessarily follows that thinking and consciousness are functions of material organisms of a special kind, are material processes on a unique qualitative level. In brief, thought is derived from matter, and not vice versa as all idealism has taught in one way or another.

Marxist scientific materialism, in accordance with these basic propositions of materialist philosophy and the data of physiology and psychology, holds that our senses with varying degrees of accuracy and adequacy reflect the world around us and that through sense-perception and reasoning we can and do achieve ever fuller knowledge of nature and its laws. There is nothing in the world that is unknowable, but only that which is not yet known.

Marxism enriches and transforms the traditional materialist approach to questions of knowledge and consciousness by two unique insights. The first of these is that our knowledge is rooted in social practice, especially that involved in production, and that both the origin and the test of the validity of our knowledge is found in the social activities required for the maintenance and reproduction of human life. The second of these insights is that just as our knowledge of nature is in the first instance determined by our productive practice so our social attitudes, theories, consciousness, is determined by the complex of our social relations. As Marx and Engels often repeated, just as being determines consciousness, social being determines social consciousness. Our thought is determined by our social environment and we can no more escape from our time and our class relations than we can from our skins.

Such is the philosophical foundation on which is built the theory and practice of Marxism or Communism as a world-wide social movement. This theory and movement, expressing originally the needs and aspirations of the industrial working class in the most advanced capitalist countries of Europe, has spread and developed until it has become the outlook and the hope of oppressed nations and peoples throughout the world. Its first aim and purpose is the establishment of the working class as the dominant class in every country. The goal of this working class power is the abolition of private property in the instruments of production and the socialization or collectivization of production on behalf of the associated producers. This is to be followed by an enormous increase in productivity, the elimination of all exploitation of man by man, of all subjection of women to men, of the distinction between physical and mental labor and that between town and country, and the achievement of full equality of all nations and peoples.

Throughout such a vast social transformation the guiding idea and ideal is that collective humanity, free from all the scars of five to seven thousand years of class rule, and all its physical and cultural limitations, can move ever forward, through its knowledge of natural and social processes, to make the world a garden in which every single human being can achieve an ever fuller and richer development of his or her capacities, in harmony with the development of all others. Basic to this is a continually increasing development of the sciences and their application to technology with a resultant increase, by leaps and bounds, of the productivity of labor.

Such is the essence of the outlook on the world and on society achieved by the great leaders of the revolutionary working class. The rise of these ideas and of working-class strength to fight for and with them, marks the emergence of mankind from its prehistoric to its historic era, to use an expression of Marx and Engels. They mean, by this phrase, that with the socialist revolution, mankind, for the first time, truly makes its own history, in the sense that it consciously plans and determines its future. In all previous society, history was, indeed, made by people, by their thought and actions. But it was made blindly, with little relation between what was intended and what was achieved.

The history of class society will always be an exciting study for the free people of the future. They will see it as a brief but vital episode in the history of the race. Lasting, at the most, from five to seven thousand years, it marked mankind's transition from an economy of scarcity, through an economy of surplus appropriated by the few, to one of abundance for all. It was the period of the rise of the arts and sciences, of technology and industry. It was the period of transition from pre-class to post-class society, from primitive tribal communal life to communism on a world scale. It was characterized by the most utter brutality and rapacity, by the incessant struggle of classes and by bloody conflicts within states and incessant wars between them. But its virtue was to pave the way for its own destruction by the development of the forces of production, and by finally producing a class that would destroy it. Mankind today stands on the threshold of a truly human world. Such is the meaning of the working-class revolution in thought and in reality.

CHAPTER III

MATTER AND MIND

MARXIST HISTORICAL materialism challenges all claims of traditional academic philosophy to pure disinterested inquiry, to above-class, self-sufficing speculation. In the same way, Engels' statement of the basic problem of all philosophy uncovers the central question without which the major part of historic philosophy would have been reduced to speechlessness.

Engels wrote: "The great basic question of all philosophy . . . is that concerning the relation of thinking and being."[1] This is the question of the relation of mind, or spirit, to nature. It is the question: which is primary, which came first, spirit or nature? In theological terms it is the question: "Did God create the world or has the world been in existence eternally?"[2] This statement, horrendous to all bourgeois contemporaries, cut away the curtain that covered philosophy through the ages. It showed the essential unity of all forms of idealism with religion, the concealment of which was the stock-in-trade of so much philosophy in the ancient slave world and since the break-up of feudal scholasticism. No longer are innumerable subtleties and equivocations possible. The question has been posed: Which comes first, matter or mind?

Engels continued: "The answers which the philosophers gave to this question split them into two great camps. Those who asserted the primacy of spirit to nature and, therefore, in the last instance, assumed world creation in some form or other . . . comprised the camp of idealism. The others, who regarded nature as primary, belong to the various schools of materialism." As long as the materialists, however, failed to understand the real nature of the question and its origin in superstition and religion, they invariably failed to see the real nature of their opponents and to combat them adequately. Now the spell is broken. The new materialism of the rising industrial working class has looked and described what it really saw. The Emperor of the Hans Andersen fairy story has no clothes!

In this statement Engels showed for the first time what most philosophy had really been about. Here is the heart of the revolution the working class wrought in philosophy. Once the basic question is defined, the complications of systems are dissolved into their essential simplicity. The basic question is that of materialism or idealism. Is the world of nature the creation of mind or spirit, or is it matter in eternal motion? Are thought or thinking and all their creations products of matter or is matter a product of thought Engels' approach reveals the identity of philosophical idealism with all religions. It matters little whether it is, "In the beginning was the Word," of the Gospel according to St. John, or the very human God of Genesis who labored six days in creating the heavens and the earth and rested on the seventh. It matters little whether it is the Absolute Idea of Hegel or the eternal forms of Plato; whether it is the ideas of Berkeley or the direct experience of Dewey—all these are so many ways of saying that mind comes first.

Naturally this insight of Engels on behalf of the new working class has annoyed the philosophical liberals no end. They seek to see some truth in idealism, some truth in materialism, and comparable errors in both, while ever opposing the recognition of the necessity to choose one or the other. Dominant today is the argument that both sides are equally "metaphysical" and can be dismissed with "a plague on both your houses."

But long before there were liberals to confuse this question, Plato had expressed an understanding of the issue with a clarity not rivalled until Engels. Plato, putting himself forward as the defender of the aristocratic-slave-owning Greek oligarchs, lashed out against the "scientific" philosophy of the merchant-artisan democratic coalitions. For Plato the previous two centuries of philosophy had a very clear meaning—they represented the struggle between an established conventional outlook and a radical scientific one. To him the issue was quite simply that "the gods exist and that they are good and honor justice" versus the determination of events by "fire and water and earth and air" with its conclusion that honor and justice are products of human life and thought.

Plato's mature position, expressed in *The Laws,* was that everything had been all right until the propagation of "the novel views of our modern scientists." These, he said, "we must hold responsible as the cause of mischief."

For the result of the arguments of such people is this—that when you and I try to prove the existence of the gods by pointing to these very objects—sun, moon, stars and earth—as instances of deity and divinity, people who have been converted by these scientists will assert that these things are simply earth and stone, incapable of paying any heed to human affairs, and that these beliefs of ours are speciously tricked out with arguments to make them plausible.[3]

What is the practical social difference between saying that mind comes first and that matter comes first? Plato is perfectly clear about this. He betrays the cause of his anxiety concerning the spread of a materialist world-view by saying, "it is of the highest importance that our arguments, showing that the gods exist and that they are good and honor justice more than do men, should by all means possess some degree of persuasiveness; for such a prelude is the best we could have in defense, as one may say, of all our laws. . . ." Here is the problem. "Our laws," our whole social system, the existing class relations, are dependent on the myths about the Gods. Aristotle said of these myths a brief generation later, that they constituted a tradition which has been added to in later times "with a view to the persuasion of the multitude and to its legal and utilitarian expediency."[4] This understanding of the meaning of the myths about the gods did not keep Aristotle from supporting them. Indeed, to the contrary, his understanding of their social function made it impossible for him to give them up. How else could Aristotle have maintained that "he who is by nature not his own but another's man, is by nature a slave."

Plato proceeds with his formidable indictment of the materialists by making the following points:

(1) They say the material world exists by "nature and chance" rather than by direction of mind.

(2) They hold that these material elements move by their own inherent nature and have thus brought into being the heavens and the earth, the plants and animals, human beings and human society.

(3) They teach that politics, or the whole structure and organization of society, is likewise due to material causes rather than to "mind" in the sense of gods controlling events.

(4.) They take the gods out of the heavens and make them the product of human imagination, of human art.

Plato's conclusion is a remarkable confirmation of Engels' statement:

> As regards the soul my comrade, nearly all men appear to be ignorant of its real nature and its potency, and ignorant not only of other facts about it, but of its origin especially,—how that it is one of the first existences, and prior to all bodies, and that it more than anything else is what governs all the changes and modifications of bodies. And if this is really the state of the case, must not all things which are akin to the soul be necessarily prior in origin to things which belong to body, seeing that soul is older than body? . . . Truly and finally, then, it would be a most veracious and complete statement to say that we find soul to be prior to body, and body secondary and posterior, soul governing and body being governed according to the ordinance of nature.[5]

Engels defined idealism as the assertion of the primacy of spirit to nature or matter. Plato finds "soul to be prior to body, and body secondary and posterior."

The most famous compromise on this question, found among some of the ancients but made central in the system of Descartes, is that neither comes first. Descartes' effort at compromise was notorious for its faultiness. He so separated mind and matter as two substances (a substance being defined as that capable of existing of itself) that he was not able to get them together to explain their interaction on either a cosmic or human level. Furthermore, he completely defeated the compromise by having to bring in a God, over and above mind and matter, to hold the two substances together. But this still meant that God, spirit, mind, the "thinking substance" is primary, and matter secondary. Thus with Descartes the "compromise" ends in making one side prior and dominant.

Spinoza, while understanding Descartes' predicament, was unable to escape completely from it. He made mind and matter not two substances, but two attributes of one substance. Then he held that this substance had infinite other attributes—thus placing mind and matter in a strange position—and he named this substance "God." His term God here had no religious value, that is, it was not a being to be prayed to, worshipped, or feared. Spinoza even identified it with nature, but not a nature that is material, but a nature of which matter is only one of infinite attributes and mind another. This peculiar position of Spinoza has puzzled students no end, even to the present day. And the controversy still goes on as to whether or not he was a materialist. Using Engels' definition, Spinoza is definitely not a materialist, because he does not make matter prior and mind secondary. Just as clearly, he is not an idealist, for mind or spirit, in his system, is decidedly not primary, not prior to matter—they are two sides of one and the same thing.

We might say that Spinoza's is the "perfect" compromise. Indeed, it is the only one that ever worked at all, with all due apologies to the "neutral monism" of our more recent empiricists and positivists.

But why not compromise? The answer falls into two parts. The first is that it could work only in the world of Cartesian physics, in a static, mechanical world. In the world of modern biological science with its teachings concerning the evolution of life and the development of the human "Mind" from the evolution of the brain and the development of society, Spinoza's position is unworkable. Natural science teaches us not that mind and matter are two sides of one and the same thing but that mind is a product of the evolution of matter; its highest product. The second difficulty in Spinoza's view is that he makes it impossible to explain the origin and function of ideas in history and society. One would have to say that it is inherent in the nature of substance, with its attributes, matter and mind, among others, that certain historical events in the physical world should have as their "obverse side" or mental counterpart, certain events in the realm of mind, certain ideas. Spinoza's theory can never explain either how ideas arise out of the material conditions of life or how they in turn can react on the material conditions and change them.

Spinoza's problems in making matter and mind co-eternal, revealed in Part II of his *Ethics,* further confirms the truth of Engels' statement that the relation of thinking and being is the great central question of all classical philosophy. He has reached a complete impasse, indicated by the fact that there has been no

genuine school of Spinozism. His was an untenable attempt
at resolving Descartes' compromise. He rejected all the traditional forms of religious and idealist thought but could not put
matter first. That required a more revolutionary break than even
the bold Spinoza could make. It was not really made, in spite
of the generally materialist approaches of Bacon, Hobbes, and
Locke, until La Mettrie in eighteenth-century France. Very
interestingly, La Mettrie himself recognized the opposition of
these two positions. He wrote: "I reduce to two the systems of
philosophy which deal with man's soul. The first and older
system is materialism; the second is spiritualism [read: "idealism"]."[6]

It is not the aim here to trace the history of materialism and
idealism. Fundamental is the question of the eternality of matter: was the world created or did it exist eternally? Before
attempting to explore this question its meaning must be clarified.
The most serious mistake to be avoided is that of identifying
nature, the world, matter, with any given structure of the universe or any known forms or modes of the existence of matter.
When Engels affirmed that the world existed eternally, he was
not referring to any given state of things. He was not talking
about the earth and the solar system, the galaxies, or the present
known forms of certain units of matter—namely, the 98 or more
elements we have discovered in nature—or the forms of energy
released by the fission or fusion of atomic nuclei. Marxists
mean, in short, by the eternality of matter, simply that matter
was neither created nor can be destroyed, but is forever under-
going, through its own inherent motion, infinite changes and
transformations.

No thought prior to Marxism was able to achieve this. The
Ionians tended to conceive water, or water-vapor, or what they
called the four elements, earth, air, water, fire, as fixed and eternal forms of matter. Democritus' atoms were eternal, fixed,
changeless units. The French materialists could not, as a rule,
escape a static notion of matter or the cosmos, and could not
avoid thinking of them as having always been that way. Kant,
in 1754, did achieve an evolutionary view of the solar system,
and Diderot somewhat later had the elements of a conception of
an ever-changing world, but it is doubtful whether even he could
envision the evolution and transformation of the elements of

matter themselves. And even to this day physical scientists who are not dialecticians seek to find the real, the basic, the permanent units of matter in specific forms and manifestations such as protons, electrons, positrons, neutrons, photons, etc.

A second difficulty of all pre-Marxist materialism was that of "establishing" or proving the eternality of matter. Either the materialists merely asserted it, merely said so, or argued for it in a negative way, a sort of "you can't prove it isn't eternal." Thus the question became a sort of "who can tell? maybe it is, maybe it isn't—you prefer to think one way, I another." The French mathematician and astronomer Laplace gave this approach its famous classical expression. Asked concerning his work, *Celestial Mechanics,* published in France at the end of the eighteenth century, why he had not referred to the deity, he answered, "I had no need of that hypothesis." This statement has, for more than a century, been hailed by "liberal" materialists as the quintessence of materialistic, iconoclastic boldness. They recognized its conformity with the progressive and scientific principle, going back to the radical English philosopher of the 14th century, William of Occam, that one shouldn't assume anything unnecessarily. They correctly understood that you don't just assume that anything is so-and-so because you want to, but only if and when some evidence requires that assumption, which is then to be tested in experience. This idea, indeed, is fundamental in the teachings of the textbooks on scientific method and logic in American colleges and universities today.

This principle has been called by various names, such as Occam's Razor (because it cuts off all unnecessary assumptions) or the law of parsimony or the principle of economy. It has been interpreted in many different ways. But behind all names for it and all interpretations, lies the notion that nature is simpler rather than more complex, and that what can be dispensed with in an explanation of phenomena can *ipso facto* be dismissed as non-existent. It is an old story that Berkeley and Hume used this principle to establish their subjective idealism. The solipsist's explanation of everything as consisting of his own sensations, a product of his own mind, is undoubtedly the simplest explanation of the world possible. It makes no "unnecessary" assumptions.

This is not the aspect of the principle, however, which con-

cerns us here. In the struggle against the scholastic philosophy
of feudalism the principle of economy served a genuinely progressive purpose, helping to eliminate all kinds of "essences,"
"forms," and other mysterious entities lurking in things. But for
the past two centuries it has had a dubious career, providing
a convenient way of escaping embarrassing questions. It has
become the technique, par excellence, of avoiding a frontal attack on any spiritualist or mystical doctrine. Since we don't
need to assume such a doctrine we can just ignore it. This
leaves the door open for any kind of idealist nonsense, without
the necessity of a positive statement or a genuine struggle against
it. Laplace was satisfied not to bring the "hypothesis" of God
into his work on the heavens. Marxist scientific materialism
must go further. For it, the question is not what one may
or may not assume, may or may not leave out, but of the total
weight of the evidence. Rather than not needing the "hypothesis" of God, Marxism finds any such assumption completely
gratuitous and anti-scientific. The question is not one of not
needing it, so much as it is one of where and how it arose and
why it has persisted.

The difference between the two approaches may be illustrated simply in relation to immortality and God. Marxists, like
all materialists from Democritus and Epicurus to the present
day, know that there is no immortality in the sense of a life
of the individual after death. As Joseph Stalin once put it:
"One cannot separate thought from matter without committing
a grave error."[7]

We know, as do all who approach the subject scientifically,
that thinking is a function of the living organism and that death
brings the dissolution of the organism and the cessation of all
consciousness. The contemporary positivist or pragmatist position, however, was clearly presented by John Dewey, when asked
for his view on the subject, in a symposium conducted by the
New York Times, in 1928. He wrote: "I have no beliefs on the
subject of personal immortality. It seems to be a subject . . .
for science rather than philosophy, or a matter of physical evidence."[8] This is nothing more than an evasion. You can not
find "*no*-souls" of people after their death, or, in other words,
no one will ever come back and report that there is nothing
beyond the grave. Using Dewey's method the liberal could

remain *safe* till the proverbial Doom's-day. It is a serious question as to whether any and all future development of science could add one iota to the evidence we now have against the actuality and possibility of survival after death.

Of course there is no way of formally *proving* that there is no immortality just as that there is no God. And here the liberal, employing Occam's Razor, rests his case. He doesn't need the assumption of God's existence. But three questions must be asked: Why was any such assumption made in the first place? Why has it persisted as an issue to the present day? What does the weight of the evidence indicate? To these questions the answers are clear and unequivocal—at least to all who wish to conceive "nature just as it exists without any foreign admixture."[9]

Firstly, the very idea of a God or gods, of spirit as primary, is a product of human ignorance under the primitive conditions of barbarism. Without this ignorance of early humans about the world that surrounded them, and of their own nature, the idea of gods would never have arisen. The God of the civilized world is, in the last analysis, the persistence in the thought of class society of the animistic approach and ideas of primitive people, of pre-class superstition concerning hidden spiritual powers in and behind all the phenomena of nature.

Secondly, we know that the idea of God has persisted through the whole of so-called civilization because it was serviceable to all exploiting classes. Just as without the ignorance of earlier people the idea of gods would never have arisen, without the needs and interests of exploiting classes, it would never have persisted.

This two-fold source of religion in the civilized world was recognized by Aristotle and expressed with extraordinary candor:

"Our forefathers in the most remote ages have handed down to their posterity a tradition, in the form of a myth, that these bodies (heavenly) are gods and that the divine encloses the whole of nature. The rest of the tradition has been added later in mythical form with a view to the persuasion of the multitude and to its legal and utilitarian expediency. . . .[10]

Thirdly, the supposition of a God or Gods runs directly counter to all science and to the whole of human experience concerning the operation of nature and society. It neither could nor would have arisen from any evidence concerning the world civilized mankind has ever discovered. The history of the arguments for God is the history of a steady retreat from one seemingly substantial citadel to another. Who today, outside of Catholic theology, would dare invoke God as "the unmoved mover," as the sole explanation of motion in the world? Where is St. Anselm's ontological argument for God? Where is the need for a non-living source of life? A mind to guide the world of animals through their life cycle? An intelligence to give order to endless galaxies?

It would be tedious to carry this further. The main point is that everything positive we know about the universe indicates a world of matter in endless transformation from one state to another, acting solely in accordance with the laws of motion inherent in it. This is the materialist position and it stands solidly opposed to all the evasions and equivocations of the "naturalists," "positivists," "pragmatists," "realists," and so on.

This is why Marxist philosophical materialism denies any God or "universal spirit." We know there is no such thing both because we understand the ignorance and class prejudice which have brought the idea to us and because everything we know about the world, the findings of every science, testify against it. We know it because all the facts of nature and social life we can obtain, indicate a world operating without purpose or forethought, aim or intention. We know that any good mankind might achieve must be achieved by its own efforts. Marxists, on the other hand, don't define themselves as "atheists." Theirs is a positive world-view and it is more logical for a scientific materialism to describe itself in positive terms than in terms that are the product of primitive mythology. How pallid, from this standpoint, is Laplace's "I had no need for that hypothesis!" Yet his statement represented the highest point reached by bourgeois philosophy and science.

We must now return to the central question of the chapter: Which came first, mind or matter; was the world created or has it existed from all eternity? There are many who profess to be materialists but who draw back at the idea of *asserting* the eternality of nature or matter. "Maybe," they like to say, "it is and maybe it isn't." "How can one possibly know whether matter

always existed or came into being at some particular time?" This
position has for some years been finding much support from the
British astronomer E. Milne, followed by others in Europe and
America, who allege to have established the creation of the
world, the "beginning" of matter, as having taken place two
billion or so years ago. Two billion years is indeed more remote
than the Judaeo-Christian five or six thousand years, but to the
materialist it is equally impossible and absurd.

The fact remains that if matter began, something must have
been there to begin it. And since that something that must begin
matter could not be matter there is nothing else for it to be but
mind or spirit. It follows, therefore, that not to assert the
eternality of matter—an assertion that all bourgeois philosophers
today teach is dogmatic and unwarranted—is to allow for the
eternality of mind. If one wants to do this, no one can stop him,
but the person who wants to think clearly, who does not want,
to use an expression of Hegel's, to "veil in mist his earthly
existence," should avoid such confusion. This hesitation about
asserting the eternality of matter is simply a form of philosophical fence-sitting, not different in kind from political and economic
fence-sitting. But such is the essence of contemporary liberalism
—waiting to see which side is certain to win before committing
itself.

But there is still another way, developed by philosophers,
of asserting the primacy of mind; another way of saying that
God made the world. And like the older and more established
way of Plato and Christianity, it, too, has its "middle" way
which is dominant in our century.

This position is known as subjective idealism to distinguish
it from the objective idealism of Plato and the older tradition. For the latter there is being or reality independent of your
mind or mine, but it is of the nature of mind or spirit, or subordinate to it. For subjective idealism thinking *is* being, or as
Berkeley succinctly expressed it, "to be is to be perceived." This
position arose in Britain early in the eighteenth century. Two
things are to be noted about its place and time of origin. One
is that it occurred in the Britain that had all but completed its
bourgeois revolution and was beginning to turn its back on the
very philosophy that had been an inseparable part of the revolution. The second thing to be noticed is that it occurs after a

tremendous revolution in science. Matter had been converted from the "pure potentiality" of Aristotle—that is, nothing in itself but capable of manifesting "form"—into a permanent, indestructible, impenetrable substance that composes everything in the universe and which obeys eternal and immutable laws. As one authority on Berkeley has observed, "Matter had only recently become a problem. . . . This elusive ghost, *Pura Potentia extra Nihil,* could never be a danger to religion, nor to anything except clear thinking."[11] Thus it was that "matter," something defined so harmlessly that it could hurt no one, had now become something to strike fear into the minds of the theologians and their intellectual supporters. The old-time religion might still be good enough for the masses, but something new was needed to save the intellectuals for idealism. As Berkeley strikingly put it, "if the arguments we have produced against it [matter] are not found equal to demonstration (as to me they evidently seem) yet I am sure all friends to knowledge, peace and religion have reason to wish they were."[12] He is saying, in other words, that maybe he cannot really prove there is no matter, but if you are a friend of peace and religion you won't ask embarrassing questions.

Berkeley upholds the priority of mind over matter through denying the existence of the latter altogether—something which even Plato and Christianity did not dream of doing. What appears to be objective and material is simply our sensations, which God gives us in regular patterns in accordance with set rules. That is his way of accounting for the orderliness of the world, its regularity. We experience the rising and setting of the sun, the alternations of summer and winter, etc., not because the earth turns on its axis and moves around the sun, but because such is the order God employs in giving us sensations. But Berkeley's was a pyrrhic victory. In one most interesting passage he complains that God in his supreme goodness and intelligence gives us our ideas in such wonderfully regular ways that instead of seeing God's hand in it we ascribe the succession of events to natural causes. The full importance of this argument has never been noted. It reveals Berkeley's true difficulty. His biggest problem is not that which is commonly supposed, namely, that his world does not hold together. You can not refute Berkeley by kicking a stone or knocking your head against the wall, by

getting hungry from not eating, or from any other single experience you can have, or act you can perform. His difficulty
is not that his "world" doesn't behave like a material one. It be-
haves too much like a material one. God, in his goodness, over-
shoots the mark: he gives us ideas exactly as a material world
would, if there were one. We can picture Berkeley wishing that
God were a bit less zealous in his care for us, so that the world
wouldn't act so in accordance with laws that people take it to
be a material world.

If it were not so tragic, if it were not so much a part of the
whole historic system of human exploitation, how ludicrous
would the whole thing be—a thinker trying to prove, immediately upon the vast successes of science from Copernicus to
Galileo and Newton, that all this vast system of the cosmos is
nothing but *ideas* in the minds of God and men! We understand
it correctly only when we see it as one more new effort, like
Plato's and so many other previous ones, to maintain that mind
or spirit is primary and matter secondary and subordinate.

The remainder of the story is easily told. It is one story
from David Hume, Berkeley's immediate successor, to Kant and
Mach, William James and John Dewey, Bertrand Russell and all
that is known today as positivism, empiricism, and pragmatism.
What Hume did with Berkeley's philosophy is similar to what
"liberals" do with every question. This is so even though Hume
was in no way a liberal. He was an extreme reactionary, so
much so that he earned from Jefferson the epithet "that degenerate son of science, that traitor to the human race." Hume *discovered* the new third way of all philosophy of the last two
centuries, the "plague on both your houses" way. Berkeley is
wrong in trying to derive our ideas from God. The materialists
are just as wrong (or Berkeley is just as wrong as the materialists) in trying to derive them from matter. We don't know
where they come from. Hume wrote: "By what argument can it
be proved, that the perceptions of the mind must be caused by
external objects, entirely different from them . . . and could
not arise either from the energy of the mind itself, or from some
other cause still more unknown to us?"[13]

The most astonishing thing about Hume's teaching is that it
has been taken for two hundred years as something other than
idealism. Today it is even called realism or naturalism. We have

just the ideas we have, it is said. We know just the things we know; things are just what they seem to be. Such an interpretation conveniently ignores one little fact, namely, that our ideas cannot, by Hume's philosophy, be referred to an objective reality. Instead of our ideas being caused by things acting on our sense organs, they are either (1) uncaused, (2) caused by the "energy of the mind itself," or (3) caused by something "unknown to us." Our ideas or sense impressions just exist and are what they are. They refer to nothing beyond themselves. My sense impression of the typewriter I am writing on *is* the real and only typewriter. It is not caused by a typewriter which exists whether I or anyone else looks at it or not. According to this Humean theory a scientific discovery is as much an invention as is the making of a new tool or gadget.

Other aspects of this Humean philosophy will be dealt with in the next chapter in connection with the theory of knowledge. What concerns us here is only the question of the relation of thinking and being. Just here is where the overwhelming majority of bourgeois philosophers fail to see what Humeanism means. Rather, they systematically exploit it as a method of attacking materialism. It cannot be understood any other way. This whole movement from Berkeley and Hume, through Kant, to neo-Kantianism, empirio-criticism, positivism, logical positivism, neutral monism, phenomenology, pragmatism, instrumentalism, operationalism, radical empiricism—it has gone and still goes under ever-changing names—has no meaning historically except as the distinctively bourgeois way of asserting the primacy of thinking over being, the subordination of matter to thought.

Plato's way of denying materialism was too obvious to serve the purpose of the bourgeois apologists. They had to deny materialism more cleverly than Plato did. His method was adequate for slave and feudal society, but capitalism with its need of science for industry and war, and with its background of anti-feudal intellectual struggles, required something far more subtle. It required a way of seeming to keep science while denying materialism. And, since the rise of communism and of Marxist dialectical materialism, it has needed ever more a way of branding as "dogmatism," "metaphysical," "old-fashioned," etc., the theory that threatens it. At our universities the very word materialism is called "old-fashioned," "a meaningless hangover from the 19th century."

Plato said "soul is prior to body, and body secondary and posterior." The bourgeois philosophers, especially in the first half of the present century, the epoch of imperialism, say "the fundamental stuff of the world is neither mental nor material but something simpler and more fundamental, out of which both mind and matter are constructed" (Bertrand Russell). Plato regarded mathematics as the highest of the sciences because it was furthest removed from matter. Einstein describes physics as dealing, like all the natural sciences, solely with "sense perceptions." "We are accustomed to regard," he says, "as real those sense perceptions which are common to different individuals, and which therefore are, in a measure impersonal."[14]

The question remains, is this way of avoiding materialism a form of idealism? In other words, is the denial of the primacy of matter an assertion of the primacy of mind, soul, or spirit? Virtually every well known philosopher of our time would deny it. Santayana even called himself a materialist, while combining Platonism and Humeanism in a fantastic hodgepodge of feudal clericalism. Russell calls himself all kinds of things, but never an idealist. The Machians as vehemently protest their innocence of idealism as did Immanuel Kant. Their contemporary descendants, the logical positivists, pride themselves in being far above the "old-fashioned" materialist-idealist controversy. John Dewey has, in two or three sentences, scattered through his scores of volumes, confessed his idealism, but then it is a true idealism as opposed, apparently, to a false one. He once wrote: "A genuine idealism and one compatible with science will emerge as soon as philosophy accepts the teaching of science that ideas are statements not of what is or has been but of acts to be performed."[15]

In this one sentence, Dewey reveals the problem of the modern bourgeois philosopher with extraordinary clarity. Not any idealism is needed, but a *genuine* one. A *genuine* idealism is compatible with science. Science teaches not what is or has been but only what to do. The missing sentence is: How can we possibly know what to do, what acts to perform, if we can't know what the world is and has been? That is Dewey's joker, and it reveals the utter degradation of the philosophy of imperialism. But it was left to a young and ingenious British student, a disciple of Bertrand Russell and a protege of John Maynard Keynes, the economist of imperialism, to say what it was all about. F. P. Ramsey wrote: "If I was to write a *Weltanschauung* [a world view] I would call it not 'What I Believe' but 'What I Feel.' . . . Philosophy does not give us beliefs, but merely relieves feelings of intellectual discomfort."[16]

Is this idealism? That is the question V. I. Lenin devoted himself to in his famous *Materialism and Empirio-Criticism*, written in 1908. He saw the issues of the bourgeois philosophy of his time, and ours, and how it was even corrupting the working-class movement of Europe and America. He saw that its main line could be summed up in the following propositions: Matter has "disappeared" as a result of new discoveries concerning the nature of the atom. Causal necessity is an old-fashioned idea to which nothing objective corresponds. All truth is purely relative. Scientists do not discover the nature of things but simply invent theories useful for organizing our sense impressions. Our sensations do not and cannot give us any knowledge of a real world. The idea of an objective reality outside our minds is dogmatic and outworn. There can be no science of society and its history.

Is this idealism? Lenin's answer is a decided Yes! This is idealism, plain and simple. And, in hundreds of pages of the most detailed scholarly analysis, Lenin tore away the veil which concealed the pure idealism underlying these philosophies. He saw that these contemporary schools were simply repeating in disguised form the doctrines of Hume, and that Hume had simply lopped off the more extravagant and expendable features of Berkeley's avowed idealism. Why bother proving God's existence, the primacy of spirit, so long as you can "refute" materialism. For then there can be no basic, radical attack on God and spirit. It is at most a question of "feeling."

Lenin saw that Hume's pretended scepticism was, in fact, nothing but a cover-up for a very positive position—anti-materialism. Hume himself had said as much. He concluded his *Dialogues Concerning Natural Religion* with the following:

A person seasoned with a just sense of the imperfections of natural reason, will fly to revealed truth with the greatest avidity. While the haughty Dogmatist, persuaded that he can erect a complete system of Theology by the mere help of philosophy, disdains any further aid, and rejects this adventitious instructor. To be a philosophical sceptic is, in a man of letters, the first and most essential step towards being a sound, believing Christian.[17]

This passage can be passed off, as it generally is, as smart-alecky double-talk revealing Hume's contempt for Christianity. Whatever he felt, however, one thing is clear: What he says is true. Whatever his private meaning, he stated in these sentences the essence of his philosophy, namely, that once the power of our senses and reason to know objective reality is denied, anything can happen, anything can be believed.

On one hand, anything can be believed. On the other, nothing can be proven. Socialism is not inevitable because it is not even inevitable that the sun will rise tomorrow. Necessity is an old-fashioned concept, as outworn as materialism. The person who *knows* that matter exists eternally is as dogmatic, for this bourgeois tradition, as the one who says God created the world. On such a framework it is easy to develop the "will to believe" of William James or the "common faith" of John Dewey. Jacques Maritain, a leading exponent today of the philosophy of St. Thomas Aquinas, has well expressed the difference between materialism and the Humeanism of the academic world. Maritain wrote of the logical positivist school that developed in Vienna as the successor of Mach's "empirio-criticism":

[It] recognizes that, outside the field proper to science, faith has a domain against which science as such has absolutely no interdict to formulate; to link science to a general atheistic conception, or to speak of a "scientific atheism," is from its point of view pure nonsense. In this it is drastically opposed to other tendencies . . . and especially to the philosophy of science proposed by dialectical materialism.[18]

And he adds: "I have said that neo-positivism leaves the door open to faith (on condition that it should not be a knowledge) and to theology (on condition that it should not be a science."[19]

This at least is clear. But what it means is that bourgeois philosophy, from Hume on, was willing to give up the luxury of proving God for the greater luxury of preventing anyone from proving the existence of matter. It was a strategic retreat which only dialectical materialism has seen through, and fought. Who could question the direct relation between Lenin's tremendous experience in the class struggle and his understanding of the real nature of contemporary Humeanism. He teaches us how to detect anti-materialist trends no matter how subtly they are disguised. He shows how to refute them by philosophical argument. But more, he exposes them as the work of the defenders of clericalism and reaction who, no longer able to gain an audience by open and avowed idealism, conceal their opposition to a scientific materialist world-view beneath a veneer of science, modernism, and perpetual open-mindedness.

No matter how you look at it, Lenin shows, these "modern" stylish trends are the work of the same ruling class. On one level, the bourgeoisie uses religion to pull the wool over the eyes of workers and farmers. On the other, it uses the blandishments of contemporary science and anti-dogmatism to deceive scientists, and professors generally, and to lead them into the anti-Marxist camp. Lenin proved that this denial of the primacy of matter was the assertion of the primacy of mind and that the argument over the existence of matter was an integral part of the class struggle.

Humeanism is idealism, regardless of its protests to the contrary. Humeans know that ideas exist, that there is thinking, consciousness, feeling. That indeed is their starting point. But matter! To assert its existence is dogmatic and unjustified. We don't know what, if anything, lies behind our sensations and consciousness. This is not neutral as between materialism and idealism. It is little wonder that this path in philosophy is closely linked in Europe and the Americas with Social-Democracy, while, at the same time, it serves as a powerful weapon of imperialism. It is the philosophy of opportunism. Many years ago a French writer, Albert Schinz, called pragmatism "a new term to designate 'Opportunism' in philosophy."[20] One could add equally well that it is also the introduction of philosophy into opportunism. But not pragmatism alone, but all forms of the philosophy of Hume do the same thing. Behind all the veneer, to the age-old question, which is prior, their answer is that of Plato: "we find soul to be prior to body, and body secondary and posterior, soul governing and body being governed according to the ordinance of nature."

The meaning of holding soul prior, and matter posterior, is the same today as in Plato's time. Ideas rule the world; things are as they ought to be. All the conflicts of our time are basically ideological. Not material forces, but ideas, determine things.

One noteworthy manifestation in our day of the idea of the primacy of mind is found in theories of advertising and propaganda. These hold that you can sell people anything if you only use the right techniques and spend enough money doing it. In the "cold war" this is expressed in the belief that the side that has the biggest transmitters will win the battle for men's minds; that if you say anything loud and long enough people will believe you. The corollary that inevitably follows is that every proposal and policy of the socialist countries is just "propaganda" and that when they win a "battle of propaganda" it is not because of any objective value in their proposals in terms of the needs and interests of the world's peoples but simply because they are somehow more clever "propagandists." In short, the material conditions of life are not primary and the ultimate determinant of human ideas, but ideas are above the material conditions, can ignore them, contradict them, or ride roughshod over them.

But among those who accept materialism today some assume that it is the advance of science alone that makes materialism credible. It follows that in earlier times idealism and openly religious positions were quite justifiable because mankind just didn't know enough to believe anything else. Such persons fail to see, first, that historically science depends at least as much on a materialist philosophy as it in turn supports it, and, secondly, that the vast growth of our knowledge of the nature of the cosmos, of matter, of protoplasm and the structure and processes of living matter, of the brain and nervous system, have not been accompanied by a growth of positive materialism. It is an appealing idea that the growth of scientific knowledge of itself dispels the clouds of mysticism and obscurantism, but it is a bourgeois liberal illusion working class thought cannot afford. It is erroneous for the simple reason that the struggle between these two main philosophical lines is not a function of actual knowledge but of social forces.

The fact is that progressive thinkers, representing progressive classes, saw the general issues of materialism versus idealism as clearly as we do, in the fourth and fifth centuries B.C. Thales and Anaximander, Anaxagoras and Empedocles, Democritus and

Epicurus were able to be basically materialist without benefit of modern science, as was Lucretius later. There were many materialists among the scientists at the museum of Alexandria under the Ptolemies (from 300 B.C. to 250 A.D.). Obviously, therefore, in spite of the tremendous achievements of natural science and the *proving* of many things that were previously only a matter of speculation, the development of science has not of itself been the decisive factor in the struggle between materialism and idealism. The position under discussion is naive because it overlooks the class struggle throughout the history of philosophy and science. Aristarchus at Alexandria developed the theory of the earth's rotation about the sun—resuscitated 1700 years later by Copernicus. Empedocles anticipated in the 5th century B.C. the natural selection theory of Charles Darwin. Democritus' atomic world-view became with Dalton, in the last century, the basis of modern chemistry.

People could be materialists, in short, in the infancy of science, and can be idealists in science's present stage. The position under criticism not only ignores these facts, but makes science something outside of the class struggle. Benjamin Farrington's *Science and Politics in the Ancient World* beautifully reveals the political nature of the struggle for and against a scientific world-view. In other words, the question of the primacy of matter *versus* mind never has been a pure question of objective evidence, of what we know or do not know about the world. It is a question ultimately, of class position. Thus it follows that idealism will disappear not through the advance of science but through the advance of society. Not new discoveries, but the advance of mankind to a classless world, spells idealism's doom.

One special aspect of the relation of thinking and being is the question of the relation of man and nature. What is man's place in the universe or in relation to the whole of nature? Traditional philosophy never could give an adequate answer to this question, but oscillated between making man everything and nature nothing, to making nature everything and man nothing. In both extremes the two were first separated and then set each over against the other.

The question is presented in innumerable ways. Was nature made for man? Is man a part of nature, in and of it, or is he something over and above it? Are we completely natural beings or is there something non-natural, supernatural, in us? Is our consciousness and knowledge a part of nature or something set over against nature? Is nature our home, the setting in which our ideas arise and our ideals must be realized, or is it something foreign, something hostile?

Plainly, these questions are simply special expressions of the question dealt with thus far in this chapter. They are, in fact, very often the main form in which the question of the relation of thinking and being manifests itself.

We might begin by taking two seemingly opposed contemporary expressions of the question. We are told, for example, how Toscanini was approached, while on a concert tour, by one of his musicians at the foot of Mount Shasta in California. He answered: "Don't speak of concerts now. Man is small—you and I and Goethe and Wagner are nothing compared with this." Toscanini had forgotten that it is for human beings alone that mountains can be superb and awe-inspiring, and also that even our attitude towards mountains as grand and magnificent, is historically conditioned. The fact seems to be that in European culture mountains such as the Alps became objects of esthetic contemplation only in the eighteenth century.

On the other side, the philosopher William E. Hocking gives the opposite position: "As compared with the mountain, the man is minute; the mountain may crush him. But the man (in so far as he is a mind) has this point of superiority, that he knows he is being crushed, whereas the mountain does not know of its own superiority. As knower of the infinity of the universe of nature, man is the greater thing."[21]

These are but two sides of the same coin. Both begin by setting man and nature over against each other—the former in order to exalt nature at man's expense, the latter in order to exalt man at nature's expense. But the problem is not which is superior, but how they were divided, in the first place, in the interest of invidious comparison.

To go back historically, we find that in the earliest Greek philosophy men first began to philosophize by treating the world as something away and apart from them. They thought they could get knowledge of it in a purely objective way, such that they, and their knowledge, had nothing whatsoever to do with the nature of the world they were knowing. It was entirely as if they and their minds were outside of the world. They forgot that they, too, were a part of the world they were knowing, and that their knowledge was a set of events or processes taking place in that world. The world they knew was a world completely outside of us human beings. A century or so later, in the development of Greek philosophy, another, an opposite development took place. Men became conscious of themselves as thinking beings and they began to center all attention not on the outer world but on their own psychology, on man's thoughts and ideas, hopes and feelings. This position, which received its classic expression in Protagoras' "Man is the measure of all things," was equally one-sided.

Interestingly, in the modern world a similar thing happened. The positions of Descartes and Spinoza, already discussed, are "compromises" between the primacy of man and the primacy of nature. And the pendulum swung for two centuries from the extreme of mechanistic materialism which either ignored man or reduced him to a machine, an automaton, to an idealism like that of Schleiermacher and Fichte which makes nature completely the product of human consciousness.

Of all the classic philosophers, Hegel came nearest a solution of the question. At least, one can say, he understood the question. But Hegel "solved" the problem in a completely perverted, or inverted, way. For him the whole material universe, of which we are a special result and, indeed, its highest product, is itself the inversion, the turning away from itself into its opposite, of the Mind, Spirit, or Reason which underlies and is all reality. This reason somehow goes out of itself and produces its other, nature, a whole physical universe. And in the development of that universe, life and human life arise, and in man this world-reason which had previously been unconscious becomes conscious of itself. In this way, for Hegel, man in knowing nature, in knowing the universe, is only mind or spirit coming to know itself.

In spite of the idealistic confusion, one thing stands out in Hegel's thought on this question. Abstractly, idealistically, he has at least broken down the dualism of man and the world. No longer is there a world of nature out there and then an inner world of human consciousness having no essential connection with it. Rather there is a total process in which self-consciousness, thinking, knowledge of the world, arise out of the whole process of the world. Man is no longer out of nature, man is no longer foreign to the universe, but is the highest phase of the universe, namely, spirit coming into consciousness of itself.

One hardly knows whether to be struck more by the perversity of Hegel's scheme or its extraordinary ingenuity. Of course, as Engels remarked, it is easy to explain how we can know the world if we make the world a creation of a reason, like ours, in the first place. Nevertheless, Hegel did try to cut through the dualism of mind and matter, man and nature, which had been the bane of virtually all previous philosophy.

Against religion and all forms of idealism the mechanical materialists tried to see man as part of nature. Nowhere was this more clearly revealed than in d'Holbach's famous *System of Nature*, published as part of the pre-revolutionary French underground intellectual movement in 1770. D'Holbach, like his confreres among the Encyclopedists, tried to make man an inseparable and integral part of nature. But his mechanistic conception of nature, as consisting of nothing but the motions of particles of matter in space, acting in accordance with the laws of mechanics, utterly prevented him from really making man natural. The metaphysical limitations of d'Holbach's materialism is shown in two paragraphs in which he makes an analogy between the movement of the particles in a whirlwind of dust or of particles of water in a storm at sea and the actions, words, thoughts, wills, passions in the persons involved in a social revolution. In both cases, equally, each motion, thought, or action of each single particle or agent is "the necessary result of the causes operating." And just as a geometrician with enough knowledge of the energies involved and the properties of each particle of dust, could demonstrate that each particle could not have acted otherwise than it did, so too could an adequate mind prove the same of every word, thought, emotion and action of the agents in "the moral whirlwind."[22]

What d'Holbach and all classic materialists, with the exception of Diderot, failed to see was that if human beings were natural, nature *must* be something more than the "accidental collocation of atoms"; that if we are natural then we must radically revise our conception of nature derived from the dualist tradition which gave man and his consciousness a separate non-natural origin. If we are natural, then consciousness, purpose, and thought, are not foreign to nature but products and manifestations of nature under specific conditions of the organization of matter. If we are natural then nature consists not only of atoms, but of molecules, cells, complex multi-cellular organisms, of brains and central nervous systems, of people and all their doings.

We human beings are as natural as uranium nuclei, as atoms, stars, galaxies. Physics is not the only science of matter, but biology, psychology, and political economy are equally sciences of nature and tell us about the nature of things, the nature of matter. There is an important sense in which a painting by a Rembrandt or Picasso is as natural as the color patterns of a butterfly's wings. There is a sense in which the symphonies of Beethoven or the operas of Mozart are as natural as the song of the mocking-bird or the indigo bunting. There is a sense in which the skyscrapers of Manhattan or "the topless towers of Ilium" are as natural as the beaver's dam or the ant hill. The romantic poet, or the naturalist (such as Henry Thoreau or John Muir), thought that when he got into the virgin woods, away from all of mankind and its doings, he was communing with nature. He failed on two counts. He forgot that the city or town he left behind him, that he "escaped" from, was natural too. He forgot that he was as natural as the trees or the birds he contemplated, and as much a product of determinate circumstances.

What has been said does not deny or ignore the distinction between human and non-human nature. That distinction is of extraordinary importance. To neglect it is to sink back into mechanical materialism: is to reduce us to the lower animals, and reduce them to the inanimate. This is the course of the exploiter in his disillusioned moments, when things are going against him. When all is rosy for the stock market or colonial investments, he is "on top of the world," above and apart from nature.

It is necessary to recognize that man and all his works are as truly a creation of nature as anything else in the world, as mountains and stars, and things like spiders' webs, birds' nests, coral, and sponges. It is equally necessary to recognize, that

man does not make things the way nature makes them outside
of man. Nature doesn't make a beaver dam the way it makes
a mountain. Nor is a skyscraper made the way a beaver dam
is. There are infinitely varied levels, in nature, of matter in
motion—infinitely varied in the complexity of their organization
and inter-relationships. The beaver does make its dam and the
hornet its nest. And man does make great cities and dams and
works of art. A gaseous nebula produces a solar system in which
life arises, and all these things occur, and they are all natural.
But man acts with a conscious purpose.

People act with an end in view, and that is what makes them
radically different from all the rest of nature. It distinguishes
them, in fact, so sharply from the rest of nature, that they traditionally thought that they were something different, something
more than natural. What they failed to understand was that
our ability to act with a purpose, to plan our future, was natural
too—natural to creatures organized with bodies like ours and
with the social history arising in connection therewith. The
philosophers who emphasized the distinction between us and
non-human nature tended towards idealism. Those who recognized our continuity with nature tended to belittle the difference and fell into mechanical materialism.

Marxism first resolved this age-old question of man's relation to nature by placing the labor process, production, as basic
to human life and central in it. This is a process in which, as
Marx stated, both man and nature participate. And it is never
a mere repetitive or one-way process. Marx says of man in
this regard: "He opposes himself to Nature as one of her own
forces, setting into motion arms and legs, head and hands, the
natural forces of his body, in order to appropriate Nature's pro-
ductions in a form adapted to his own wants. By thus acting
on the external world and changing it, he at the same time
changes his own nature."[23]

Some academicians might answer at this point that in our
times they have solved this problem. Naturalism, indeed, is
quite a respectable philosophy, as can be seen from the volume
Naturalism and the Human Spirit,[24] but the editors of this volume tell us that their distinction from other philosophical positions lies more in what they reject than in any positive position
they take about the universe. This is truly a "shame-faced ideal-

ism." They want some of the intellectual luxuries that come with the honesty and openness of scientific materialism, but without its professional, social, and political liabilities.

John Dewey is claimed to be something of a naturalist, as one who makes men at home in nature. But a careful examination of his most important single work, *Experience and Nature*, reveals a completely idealist position. He identifies nature with collective human experience. We do not, according to Dewey, experience nature but our experience *is* nature; nature is our *experience*. This is a case of unabashed idealism and is Dewey's own special way of denying that nature exists objectively to us and causes our experience—a particular way of asserting that thinking is prior to being. No more striking proof of the fraudulence of Dewey's "naturalism" can be found than in his refusal to answer the question Morris R. Cohen asked him as to whether he believed the earth existed prior to man.

Bertrand Russell has posed for nearly sixty years as something not too far from a materialist (neutral at worst). But in one of his earlier essays, "A Free Man's Worship," he revealed his philosophical technique to be the old one of exploiting the weaknesses of mechanical materialism in order to buttress subjective idealism. His thesis runs like this: modern science presents us with a world void of meaning and purpose. It teaches that:

[Man's] origin, his growth, his hopes and fears, his loves and beliefs, are but the outcome of accidental collocations of atoms; that no fire, no heroism, no intensity of thought and feeling, can preserve an individual life beyond the grave; that all the labors of the ages, all the devotion, all the inspiration, and the noonday brightness of human genius, are destined to extinction in the vast death of the solar system.[25]

This is a pathetically juvenile reaction against orthodox religion. Russell has discovered, with horror, that there is no God and no life after death, and he throws up his hands in despair. He continues speaking of "such an alien and inhuman world," of "Nature, omnipotent but blind," as if the matter that produced mankind was *inhuman*, as if nature was something against and foreign to us. And what is Russell's conclusion? What do we do in this alien and inhuman world, in this brutal nature acting without concern for our desires?

Having created this horrible opposition between man and nature, Russell solves the problem—solves it by still further defiance, and an obsolete dichotomy between force and ideals. It will be worth quoting his concluding passages entire:

When, without the bitterness of impotent rebellion, we have learned not to resign ourselves to the outward rule of Fate and to recognize that the non-human world is unworthy of our worship, it becomes possible at last so to transform and refashion the unconscious universe, so to transmute it in the crucible of imagination, that a new image of shining gold replaces the old idol of clay. . . .

Brief and powerless is Man's life; on him and all his race the slow, sure doom falls pitiless and dark. Blind to good and evil, reckless of destruction, omnipotent matter rolls on its relentless way; for Man, condemned today to lose his dearest, tomorrow himself to pass through the gate of darkness, it remains only to cherish, ere yet the blow falls, the lofty thoughts that ennoble his little day; disdaining the coward terrors of the slave of Fate, to worship at the shrine that his own hands have built; undismayed by the empire of chance, to preserve a mind free from the wanton tyranny that rules his outward life; proudly defiant of the irresistible forces that tolerate, for a moment, his knowledge and his condemnation, to sustain alone, a weary but unyielding Atlas, the world that his own ideals have fashioned despite the trampling march of unconscious power.[26]

Thus does one of the leading philosophers of our century represent the relation of man and nature. Obviously, it is not the relation of man to nature Russell is talking about at all, but the relation of man to man. Equally obvious, is his determination to resist social change, to retreat, into "the world his own ideals have fashioned." This is only a shallow pretense of materialism. It is idealism from beginning to end. First he creates a completely mechanistic "inhuman" nature, then he, its offspring, "proudly" defies it. Marxism has an entirely different conception of nature and of man's place in it.

Another example, from a prominent American thinker, exhibits the same bankruptcy. The psychoanalyst, Eric Fromm, similarly opposes man to nature and nature to man, and then seeks a *reconciliation* in resignation. Fromm, however, has new angles, new subtleties. For him, man was originally, in his primitive state, at home with nature. It was his reason that was his blessing but "also his curse." "Man is the only animal," Fromm writes, "that can be *bored*, that can be *discontented*, that can be evicted from paradise. . . ."[27]

After much more of the same thing, Fromm concludes: "There is only one solution to his problem: to face the truth, to acknowledge his fundamental aloneness and solitude in a universe indifferent to his fate. . . ." Again we see the same senseless and stupid separation from nature, followed by a false reconciliation. Here it is man's mind or reason that is at fault. The implication is, as for Nietzsche, Bergson, and existentialism, that if only we had not started thinking, not developed our distinctive human reason, our problems in relation to nature would never have arisen. As with Bergson, our use of thought rather than instinct was our "original sin."

Fromm's approach, like that of Russell, is not an expression at all of the difficulties of man's relation to his natural environment, to the nature of which he is a part, but of the decadence and hopelessness of bourgeois society.

These are only two contemporary illustrations of the general historic failure to conceive correctly our relation to nature. The root of this failure lies, of course, in the impossibility of exploiting society to understand the role of labor in relating man to nature, the role of the production process in making men themselves and their history. Marx and Engels, while ridiculing those who mechanically separate man and nature, also made fun of those who unify them idealistically. "The celebrated 'unity of man and nature,'" they wrote, "has always existed in industry and has existed in varying forms in every epoch according to the lesser or greater development of industry, just like the 'struggle' of man with nature, right up to the development of his productive powers on a corresponding basis."[28]

Marx and Engels believed that it was precisely the neglect of this real basis of history that caused it to be written "according to an extraneous standard; the real production of life seems to be beyond history, while the truly historical appears to be separated from ordinary life, something extra-superterrestrial. With this the relation of man to nature is excluded from history and hence the antithesis of nature and history is erected."[29]

This is an extraordinary illustration of the revolution in thought wrought by the philosophers of the modern working class. No previous philosophy could explain or understand man's relation to nature, because it could not see the production process as the material basis of human life. It looked upon the relation of man and nature *theoretically,* conceiving it in terms of contemplation or speculation. The ideologists of class society, Marx wrote, represent

the relations of man and nature from the very outset not as practical relations—i.e., those founded on action, but as *theoretical*—but people never
begin under any circumstances with "standing in theoretical relationship
with objects." . . . Like other animals, they begin by *eating* and *drinking,*
etc.—i.e., they do not "stand" in any relationship, but *function actively,* with
the help of their actions take possession of certain objects of the outside
world, and in this way satisfy their requirements.[30]

As the whole theme of the present volume indicates, this approach is what no bourgeois philosopher dare take without
changing his class relations and hence ceasing to be a bourgeois
philosopher. Labor is the key to the relation of man and nature.
Those who do the work of the world find neither a romantic
benevolent "over-soul" in the nature they struggle with, nor "an
alien and inhuman world." They find external nature recalcitrant
and yet amenable to being worked up for human purposes. The
soil is hard but the tractor-pulled plough easily cuts through
it. Rain sometimes tragically fails to come in time for the crops
on which our life depends, but we can build dams and canals
and through irrigation rise above the level of dependency on
natural processes. As the Soviet horticulturist, Michurin, liked
to put it, "We must not wait for nature's favors, but wrest them
from her." From this standpoint there is neither a hostile nature
nor a kindly one. Man is not separated and divided from nature,
but, through a knowledge of her laws, can change her course
to serve his purposes.

It was Frederick Engels who carried this conception of our
relation to nature to its highest level. Engels felt immensely
at home in the universe. He despised all dualisms which made
a sharp and unbridgeable separation of man and nature, as of
mind and matter. If man is a natural product of this material
world, Engels reasoned, then he truly belongs to it. He is that
animal "in which nature attains consciousness of itself."[31] Furthermore, if nature or matter produced man this once that we
definitely know of, in our little corner of the universe, it certainly
is able to have done it many times before and to do it many
times again. Man on this earth has a beginning and an end, but
Engels believed, in full cognizance of all the accidents in-

volved, that by the same necessity which caused life and man to arise here, it must happen elsewhere too. For whatever matter is, it can and does under certain conditions produce life and thinking beings, and these are as truly revelatory of its nature as are stars and atoms.[32]

Never, before Marx and Engels, has a thinker so fully and clearly seen man as natural and nature as material. The philosophers either took man out of nature and set him over against it or they made nature anthropomorphic by attributing human desires and purposes to the world as a whole. When they did not deify the world, they either wrote it off as hostile to man, or wrote man off as insignificant in the world.

One passage of Engels on the subject should be quoted in full:

> Thus at every step we are reminded that we by no means rule over nature like a conqueror over a foreign people, like someone standing outside nature—but that we, with flesh, blood, and brain, belong to nature, and exist in its midst, and that all our mastery of it consists in the fact that we have the advantage over all other beings of being able to know and correctly apply its laws.
>
> And, in fact, with every day that passes we are learning to understand these laws more correctly, and getting to know both the more immediate and the more remote consequences of our interference with the traditional course of nature. . . . But the more this happens, the more will men not only feel, but also know, their unity with nature, and thus the more impossible will become the senseless and anti-natural idea of a contradiction between mind and matter, man and nature, soul and body, such as arose in Europe after the decline of classic antiquity and which obtained its highest elaboration in Christianity.[33]

In this way does the thought of the industrial working class not only put an end to futile and mistaken speculation concerning our place in nature, but raises the question to an entirely new level. Man's unity and harmony with nature is no longer a problem of theory to solve, but an endless goal for practice to move towards. In this approach there is neither the pessimism of the disillusioned nor the false optimism of those who believe that nature outside of us is working for our purposes. There is only the ever-developing scientific knowledge of what is possible to us and the will to make this earth a fitting abode for the ever fuller development of the extraordinary creatures it has produced.

Thus in practice are resolved the age-old questions of the relation of nature to man and of matter to mind. Collective mankind transforms the earth to suit its purpose and, paradoxically, proves the priority of matter to mind in the very process of making nature serve human ends. In the famous words of Francis Bacon, "Nature to be commanded must be obeyed." And we can add: man can control nature only through an understanding of nature's primacy and the knowledge of its laws.

CHAPTER IV

KNOWLEDGE, PRACTICE AND REALITY

THERE IS no better criterion of the progressive or reactionary character of a society than its attitude towards knowledge or science. Is knowledge good? Should we have more of it? Is it necessary and desirable for social well-being? Is it capable of unlimited expansion and development? Or are there limits to human knowledge? Is it a dangerous thing? Do we have too many scientists and too few "men of God?" Does knowledge distract us from higher, spiritual pursuits? Should knowledge or science be contrasted with "wisdom" as something inferior?

On the plane of professional philosophy these simple questions become expressed in varied sophisticated forms. Does knowledge come from experience? Is our knowledge real and does it really reflect the world around us? Is practice the origin and test of knowledge? Is the process of acquiring knowledge a purely natural one, standing in no need of God and revelation? Is there an "unknowable," forever removed from all possible scientific understanding?

All of these questions which have been so debated for some 2,500 years, and the issues of which are more or less directly related to the struggles of classes, come down to one basic question: can man, through the methods of the sciences, acquire such knowledge of nature and society as will enable him to control them for his purposes? There is only one way, historically evolved, of course, of answering this question positively. But there are innumerable ways of denying it; of converting knowledge from a developing fact into a problem.

It is the hardest thing for the ordinary working-class person to understand that for so much of our modern philosophy knowledge is a "problem," and its objectivity is doubted or denied by the dominant contemporary philosophical schools. Nothing

81

more clearly reveals the bankruptcy of bourgeois society in its imperialist epoch than does its approach to the question of knowledge. But it shares its difficulties concerning knowledge with most previous social eras, save for those relatively few and brief periods of the ascendancy of a new class that was able to carry society forward by revolutionary contributions to the forces and relations of production.

In the course of human history knowledge has been converted, by reactionary classes, from a fact of our world into a problem that becomes increasingly insoluble. From the closest actual relationship to practice, knowledge has been removed to a sphere of especially rarefied theory. From a process as natural as eating and drinking and producing food and clothing, knowledge has been converted into a mystery requiring special divine illumination, or special faculties in man not derived from his earthly constitution. From a reflection in our minds of the nature of things, of the world around us, it is converted into a veil or screen, separating us helplessly from whatever mysterious "what-not" might be outside our heads. Such are the "achievements" of the philosophy of reactionary ruling classes with respect to a basic pre-condition of any *human* life whatsoever, namely our ability to reflect, through sensation and thought, our objective surroundings.

Whereas for so much previous philosophy knowledge was a "problem" to be solved, for Marxism it is a fact to be advanced. Only twice before in history was there a comparably healthy approach to knowledge. These were, in the Western world, from the Ionian philosophers of Greece through Democritus and Aristotle to the scientists of the Museum of Alexandria, and during the two or three centuries of the break-up of feudalism and the rise of capitalism. This does not mean that new knowledge of the properties of things and of improved tools and instruments of production was not almost constantly being acquired. It means only that the dominant modes of thought were such as to discourage, limit, or deny knowledge in the interests of a ruling class which feared the growth of knowledge as a threat to its social rule. Such a class seeks invariably to circumscribe knowledge within carefully defined boundaries, or to banish it altogether. A declining class bemoans knowledge and science as a cause contributing to its decline. A rising class produces a Francis Bacon with his magnificent vision that it is not knowledge that has failed but that society has failed to acquire the knowledge possible to it and to use such knowledge for human advancement.

The social preconditions for an objective scientific approach to knowledge are readily definable. In class society it requires a class that needs and wants knowledge to advance itself as a class. It requires a class that needs knowledge to fulfill its interests more than it needs existing traditions and superstition to maintain its class supremacy. These conditions can be fulfilled only when: (1) there is a sharp contradiction between the existing economic relations and the growing forces of production confined within them; and (2) a class exists whose position in society is such that its interests can be served only by its development of the forces of production. These conditions have been realized only a few times in history, but never so decisively and unequivocally as with the modern proletariat, through which these conditions are realized in a qualitatively new way.

There has been a "problem" of knowledge only because there is a class struggle, only because there are socially-determined enemies of knowledge. The so-called problem of knowledge, the whole of classic knowledge theory or epistemology, directly reflects in itself the struggle between exploiting classes which needed ancient myths and superstition derived from pre-class society, and rising classes which need knowledge for greater mastery of the world.

Frederick Engels, in his discussion of the relation of thinking and being as the basic question of all philosophy, stated that the question has yet another side: "In what relation do our thoughts about the world surrounding us stand to this world itself? Is our thinking capable of cognition of the real world? Are we able in our ideas and notions of the real world to produce a correct reflection of reality?"[1]

This is, of course, not the only question concerning knowledge, but it is the most fundamental and far-reaching one. In classic philosophy the tendency has been to make the question of whether our knowledge is derived from sense experience (empiricism) or from the mind itself (rationalism) the most important question. Again, one of the subjects for popular debate in philosophical circles in our century is that of probability.

"Certainty," say our pragmatist contemporaries, "is an old-fashioned idea." They speak only of degrees of probability and convert it into an absolute. Further, learned discussions are written on the nature of error, which, instead of being human supposedly presents some kind of mystery. One might say of the academic philosophers today that with regard to knowledge they prefer to deal with everything but the one real question: do we have real knowledge of the real world?

The idealists have always sought to make a mystery of knowledge when they did not deny it altogether. Their ways of doing both are varied and exceedingly ingenious, and will be gone into shortly. From Plato to Hume, Kant, or Bergson they have found ways of denying that we can have knowledge of the world about us in space and time through either sense experience or reason or both. There is, for them, either no real world to know or it is a world penetrable only through revelation, intuition, mystic experience—anything but ordinary sense experience and its organization through those processes of thought common to all normal human beings.

But to most philosophers in the period of imperialism, all the openly idealist positions are "old-fashioned" and "dogmatic." They have a cleverer way, they think, of denying that we can know the real world, and that is by denying that there is any such thing—by denying that there is anything beyond our experience and knowledge to which they refer and which they more or less adequately reflect. These are the positivists and the pragmatists.

The central purpose for doing this is to deny (1) that the process of production and its attendant technology and science is the only way of knowledge and the only path to the understanding of the world, and (2) that there can be through productive labor and social practice and the experience and reason attendant upon them, such knowledge of the world of nature and society as enables us to change them for our purpose. Does it need to be argued that in both cases this denial represents the position and need of an exploiting class that lives on the labor of others and which fears change?

The pre-Marxist materialists, with the best will in the world, still failed to account for and explain the knowledge we have because, as Mao Tse-tung has said. they left "man's social nature and historical development out of account." As a result of this failure they could not "explain the dependence of cognition upon social practice—its dependence upon production and class struggle."[2] Not being able to see sense experience, inference and judgment as practical human activity, as inseparable from the productive process and all social life, they were unable to explain how knowledge arose, the processes by which it developed, and how we can and do employ it in changing the world.

But before analyzing the limitations of pre-Marxist materialism, limitations it had in spite of all "good intentions," we should deal with the distinctly idealist approaches. Of these, the most fundamental and far-reaching in influence is that of Plato and Platonism. Here we find a way of so circumscribing man's knowledge as to render it completely incapable of trespassing on the sacred precincts of mythology and superstition.

For Plato and the whole Platonic tradition, which includes so much of all Western philosophy, Jewish, Christian and Moslem, we do know a reality. But what they claim to know is a fraudulent reality, spelled with a capital "R"—a world of forms or essences, completely remote and opposed to the world of daily life and toil.

Plato first transforms all the concrete material things of our world—tables and beds, horses and dogs, into abstract *forms* of these things—into tabularity, bedness, horsiness, and dogitity. Then, all actual tables and beds, horses and dogs, gotten rid of, it is easy for Plato to establish that we know their *form* only through the mind or intellect itself, conceived as completely divorced from the body and its sense organs. Having achieved this feat, Plato argues that the senses are hindrances rather than aids to knowledge, and that the "higher" the knowledge, the more we know the forms or essences of things, the less we know about their concrete particularity, about all their actual manifestations. To know about horses, for example, is to know horsiness or horséity—the form or essence of horses—rather than to know anything real and concrete about the varieties of horses on earth, their various capabilities and usages, their evolutionary development, and the like. The old gag that the academician is one who knows "more and more about less and less" needs to be inverted for Plato. His method allows us to know *less and less about more and more*, until we finally arrive at the knowledge of pure being, the form of forms, or, in other words, pure nothingness.

Nothing, however, betrays Plato's anti-materialist attitude better than his denial of the role of the senses in acquiring knowledge. Two passages from Plato's dialogue on the death of Socrates tell the story:

> If we are ever to know anything absolutely, we must be free from the body and behold the actual realities with the eyes of the soul alone. . . . While we live we shall be nearest to knowledge when we avoid, so far as possible, intercourse and communion with the body, except what is absolutely necessary, and are not infected by its nature, but keep ourselves free.
>
> Then when does the soul attain truth? . . . And he attains to the purest knowledge of them who goes to each of them with the mind alone, not allowing when in the act of thought the intrusion or introduction of sight or any other sense in the company of reason, but with the very light of the mind in her clearness, searches into the very truth of each; he has got rid, as far as he can, of eyes and ears and of the whole body, which he conceives of only as a disturbing element, hindering the soul from the acquisition of truth when in company with her. . . .[3]

Thus it is that the greatest ideological spokesman of ancient slave society, not unlike his Egyptian forebears, or the Christian slave-owners and feudal lords to follow, makes knowledge independent of the body, independent of matter. In making knowledge the function of a "pure" disembodied mind, he is expressing his class's contempt for the body as serviceable only for manual labor. He is expressing that division of labor in society which came with the production of a surplus over the bare needs of daily life and which became the basis for, and was further sharpened by a class of expropriators of the common property. He is expressing the fact that the separation of mind and matter, as two separate substances, arises out of the division of manual and intellectual labor in early class society.

Thus the Platonic theory of knowledge both reflects the existing class relations and becomes a justification for the slave-owning class. While the slaves and artisans use their bodies in dealing with material things, their masters employ their minds in dealing with higher, spiritual things—with a reality beyond and above the material world. Plato's was not a theory of knowledge but a sanctification of exploiting society. And although it has been largely superseded in the bourgeois world with a philosophy better adapted to the needs of an industrial society,

it still permeates thinking in the arts, in mathematics, and pene-
trates deeply into the thinking of college educated people in
the contemporary world. It is clear that the present split of
mind and body, of knowledge and labor, is not simply the continuation of the Platonic tradition but is the ideological reflection of a society as much divided into conflicting classes as was
that of Plato.

Plato's theory of mathematics has been especially persistent
in learned circles. For him, following the earlier and ultra-
reactionary Pythagorean philosophy, mathematics was the highest of the sciences because it dealt with pure forms alone, divorced completely from matter. And whereas Plato disparaged
the other sciences, he glorified mathematics as completely the
product of mind and freed from any dependence on the senses.

It needs only to be mentioned that Aristotle, in relation to
knowledge as to every other question, compromised with Plato's
position. He sought to soften its more obviously objectionable
features but still retained its essence. He had to admit the role
of the senses in knowledge, but then took the sting out of the admission by inventing a special form of the intellect, the so-called
"active intellect," which knew all the higher things and which
was independent of the body and its senses.

Aristotle had an extraordinary sense of the desire people have
for knowledge and especially sense-experience. "Everyone de-
lights to know," he liked to say. Yet he was led by his class
relations to make *doing* a function of slaves, and *knowing* that
of masters. He admits that the knowledge the master requires
for his "superintendence" of slaves "is not anything great or
wonderful; for the master need only know how to order that
which the slave must know how to execute." And he adds with
delightful frankness: "Hence those who are in a position which
places them above toil have stewards who attend to their
households while they occupy themselves with philosophy or
with politics."[4] Marx noted this passage because it revealed
a process also taking place under the capitalism of his time—that
by which more and more the labor of "superintendence" is divorced from ownership (a separation deliberately blurred today
by the word "management" which ambiguously covers both
relations).

Here, in the knowledge theory of Plato and Aristotle, is the great classic justification for a ruling class. The slave owner, through his ownership of slaves, requiring knowledge that is admittedly not "anything great and wonderful," can then be free from the necessity of manual labor in order to pursue the intellectual activities of mankind, either in philosophy or politics. This applies to the capitalist as well, but it was precisely the development of capitalism which put an end to any possible justification for a special owning class to do the intellectual work of society. Engels beautifully expressed this fact, on behalf of the modern working class, in his essay on *The Housing Question*:

> It is precisely this industrial revolution which has raised the productive power of human labor to such a high level that—for the first time in the history of humanity—the possibility exists, given a rational division of labor among all, to produce not only enough for the plentiful consumption of all members of society and for an abundant reserve fund, but also to leave each individual sufficient leisure so that what is really worth preserving in historically inherited culture—science, art, human relations —is not only preserved, but converted from a monopoly of the ruling class into the common property of the whole of society, and further developed. And here is the decisive point: as soon as the productive power of human labor has developed to this height, every excuse disappears for the existence of a ruling class. Was not the final reason with which class differences were defended always: there must be a class which need not plague itself with the production of its daily subsistence, in order that it may have time to look after the intellectual work of society? This talk, which up to now had its great historical justification, has been cut off at the root once and for all by the industrial revolution of the last hundred years. The existence of a ruling class is becoming daily more and more a hindrance to the development of industrial productive power, and equally so to science, art and especially cultural human relations. There never were greater boors than our modern bourgeois.[5]

Only two major positions on knowledge were developed during the rise of the capitalist world. These were necessary because Platonism and Aristotelianism as the major forms of ideology of European feudalism were equally hostile both to the ideology necessary for bourgeois power and to the needs of developing technology and industry. Both new positions had progressive aims and proceeded from what were basically meant to be materialist positions. The first, historically, was that of rationalism given its classic formulation by Descartes in the first half of the seventeenth century. The second, empiricism, received its definitive formulation at the hands of the English physician and political thinker, John Locke, near the end of the same century.

These two theories of the knowledge process have played such an important role, practically and theoretically, that they need to be dealt with in some detail. This is especially so because to this day rationalism and empiricism are frequently represented as alternatives between which we must choose. It was one of the striking features of Marxist philosophy that it was the first to see these positions as false, because one-sided. Rationalism, as the teaching that knowledge comes through reason or thought rather than through sense experience, tends to belittle experience and observation. Empiricism, as the teaching that all knowledge comes from our senses was distorted into the teaching that reason cannot be trusted and that our knowledge is limited to what our senses directly perceive. As we shall see, both failed to start with and build upon practice, especially as involved in the process of production and in actual daily human relations.

Descartes, a Catholic, was educated in Jesuit schools but early rebelled against the barrenness of scholastic philosophy. He earnestly sought the advancement of knowledge. He had an extraordinarily keen perception of the kind of knowledge artisans and other workers had and he contrasted this with the Aristotelianism of the colleges and universities. Also, he had a most progressive idea of what human life could do with such knowledge, even going so far as to declare that when we had the kind of knowledge of all the bodies that surround us "as distinctly as we know the various crafts of our artisans, we might also apply them in the same way to all the uses to which they are adapted, and thus render ourselves the lords and possessors of nature."[6]

But in spite of these positive features, Descartes made two fatal errors. First, in his revolt against the traditionalism, dogmatism, and authoritarianism of the feudal scholastic philosophy, he fell into an individualism which made the individual, conceived as a perfect and complete expression of pure mind, the sole and absolute judge, in short, he divorced knowledge from the society in which alone it arises and exists, and made it a kind of personal property. I may not know anything else but I know that *I* exist and have the ideas I have.

Secondly, as a result of his separation of mind and matter as
described in the preceding chapter, Descartes was inevitably
led to make knowledge of the outer world dependent on God
rather than on collective human experience. Or, to put it another
way, instead of our common experience and practice proving
the validity of our knowledge, Descartes requires God to guarantee the truth of our experience. He asks such questions as:
How can I trust my senses? How can I know that they do not
fool me? How do I even know that I have a body? Maybe there
is a malevolent demon who deliberately deceives me, giving me
all these sensations of people and things when really they do not
exist at all. Thus, both because Descartes still needed to keep
a God and because of his dualism of matter and mind, he sets
the stage for making belief in God the precondition for believing that we have knowledge of the objective world. Without belief in a God who would not deceive us, we could trust neither
the evidence of our senses nor the conclusions of our reason.

It is very possible that Descartes prided himself on this
achievement of using God to prove that he could trust his senses
and that through them and his reason he could get ever more
knowledge of the real world. Against Platonism, he was using
God to justify our senses and the doctrine that through them we
acquire knowledge. Against Aristotelianism he was using God
to establish that the world was *material* and that knowledge was
knowledge of bodies and the laws of their motion. It is certain,
however, that this compromising approach of Descartes could
not escape the pitfalls of the Platonic tradition, nor could it establish knowledge as a natural, material process. His timidity,
largely representative of his class, brought in its wake twin evils
which did lasting damage. One was the hopeless separation
of mind and matter, thinking and being, that required a God
to get them together again. The second was the dependence
on God and our belief in him to guarantee the validity of our
knowledge.

Thus with Descartes, as with most of the Christian tradition,
we must believe in God before we can legitimately believe in
anything else. And although the Catholic Church has in general
opposed Descartes to this day, the fact is that in his knowledge
theory, knowledge of nature is subordinated to belief in God.
Seeking to free science from the feudal church and its teachings,

he nonetheless made science subordinate to theology. He sought to establish that through knowledge we can "become the lords and possessors of nature," but he then so separated nature and *mind* that he had to make knowledge dependent on faith. He sought to establish that knowledge was achieved through, and expressed by, the practice of workers. Instead he removed it from the world of matter altogether, and made it a function of a purely spiritual substance.

It would be easy to dismiss Descartes as a bundle of contradictions. Many subsequent thinkers did that and then accepted John Locke's theory of knowledge without question. But Locke, the ideological leader of the British bourgeoisie, compromised every bit as much as Descartes and like him ended in a host of contradictions which later reactionary thinkers could use for purposes opposite to those of both Locke and Descartes. The explanation for the similar contradictions in two thinkers of widely differing backgrounds and apparently completely opposed approaches can be accounted for only by the class relationships through which they operated, the level of scientific knowledge of the time (Locke had the advantage of doing his philosophical work nearly forty years after Descartes did his), and the intellectual or philosophical tools they had to work with. The first is of course the most decisive influence in that it determined how they utilized the scientific knowledge available and how they employed the philosophical heritage they had received. It also alone explains the similarity of their conclusions in the light of the opposition of their premises.

In the traditional academic teaching, Descartes and Locke are represented as standing in absolute opposition. Descartes is called a rationalist, Locke an empiricist. But they had in common both their aims and their errors, and the two traditions fused, as Marx observed, in the most radical thought ever produced on behalf of a class that sought to be a new exploiting class, that of the French materialists of the eighteenth century. It is to be noted that Descartes came in a far less advanced stage of the development of the bourgeoisie than did Locke, who was actually one of the bourgeois revolution's leading political as well as philosophical exponents.

John Locke provides the most illuminating lessons in the history of philosophy concerning knowledge theory. Few mistakes are possible that he didn't make, few dead ends he did not stray into. He was a modest man, who declared in the preface to his vast treatise on knowledge theory, *Essay Concerning Human Understanding,* that in an age which produces such masters in the sciences as a Boyle or a Huygens or a Newton, "it is ambition enough to be employed as an under-laborer in clearing the ground a little, and removing some of the rubbish that lies in the way to knowledge." Further, Locke was a practical man with a vast contempt for abstract metaphysical speculation. But his practicality was narrow, the practicality of a class that wanted only one thing—power for the purpose of making money. Consequently, Locke wanted to show his contemporaries that we can get all the knowledge we need for our purposes, but in doing so he made the irretrievable error of assuming an unknowable.

Locke wrote: "We shall not have much reason to complain of the narrowness of our minds, if we will but employ them about what may be of use to us; for of that they are very capable; and it will be an unpardonable, as well as childish peevishness, if we undervalue the advantages of our knowledge, and neglect to improve it to the ends for which it was given us, because there are some things that are set out of the reach of it."[7] Locke nowhere tells us precisely what *things* are "set out of the reach" of our knowledge, but before he is through with his treatise he makes the startling "discovery" that it is objective reality, matter, the cause of our sensations, which is out of the reach of our knowledge.

Maurice Cornforth, in his valuable book, *Science and Idealism,* to which the reader should refer, has most ably analyzed in a few pages the inconsistencies and difficulties in Locke's knowledge theory. It is necessary here simply to uncover the basic orientation or approach that was deep-seated in the whole of classic philosophy and which created a *problem* of knowledge of such a kind that no solution was possible.

It is a most interesting experience to follow Locke's struggles in the fourth and final part of his *Essay.* He is trying valiantly and most desperately to insist that our senses give us real knowledge of the real world, of the world outside our minds. He had already shown how things acting on our senses cause sensations or ideas to be produced in our minds. He had watched, as if from outside, the ideas getting into a person's mind from the action of things on his sense organs. When all the ideas are in, then Locke goes into the mind he had been observing—*and closes the door behind him.* Now he finds the mind certainly well furnished with ideas of every variety and description. But how can he know now that there is anything outside corresponding to these ideas? All we can possibly do, he insists, is to compare and contrast our ideas. He concludes that obviously "our knowledge is only conversant about them."

Through chapter after chapter, Locke wrestles with this problem. Our knowledge must go beyond our ideas, yet how can it, when only ideas are the "immediate" objects of our knowledge? "It is evident," he writes, "the mind knows not things immediately, but only by the intervention of the ideas it has of them. Our knowledge, therefore, is real only so far as there is a conformity between our ideas and the reality of things." But how can we possibly tell if there is such a conformity or not, Locke asks. He hedges, stalls, compromises. And he was absolutely right in doing so, for as he had set up the problem there was no solution. Finally, in one extraordinary passage, he says that we can't *know* the things outside us, but we have "an assurance that deserves the name of knowledge."[8] For if, he says, we can persuade ourselves that our senses don't deceive us, "it cannot pass for an ill-grounded confidence." This means little more than that if we can succeed in persuading ourselves we will be persuaded. Anyway, he's not going to argue with anyone who is so sceptical as to doubt the existence of the things he sees and feels, for what would be the use, "since he can never be sure I say anything contrary to his own opinion." Then, trying to clinch his point, Locke employs an argument which destroys his own "common sense" and initially materialist approach. He says: "As to myself, I think God has given me assurance enough of the existence of things without me; since, by their different application, I can produce in myself both pleasure and pain, which is one great concernment of my present state."[9] How God gets into this argument is difficult to see, but it is not without significance that Locke ends where Descartes began. The first needed God to begin his analysis of knowledge, the second needed God to conclude it.

Two things here are especially noteworthy. One is the discrepancy between Locke's bold starting point and aim, namely, to prove that knowledge is a natural process that begins with things operating on our sense-organs, and his pathetically timid conclusion, that we must try to persuade ourselves, with God's help, that we can trust our senses and have any knowledge of the world outside us. Some bourgeois scholars have seen this discrepancy. None has been particularly concerned with, nor successful in, explaining the reasons for it. The second thing to be noted has again been almost entirely ignored by the academic philosophers. That is the basic similarity between Locke and Descartes who appear so opposite.

Why were these two very different thinkers of different countries and national traditions completely unable to achieve a solid theory of knowledge? They were both progressive. They stood squarely in the camp of advancing science and notably aided its advancement. They sought to extend human knowledge and mankind's mastery of the world. They were exceedingly talented individuals, great men. Yet they failed to achieve their goal, even though they pursued apparently completely opposed paths.

Neither Descartes nor Locke, two of the greatest figures of bourgeois philosophy, could see knowledge as a social process. They saw it only in their own individual heads. Each could have written the words of Bertrand Russell, Locke's anachronistic follower: "Theory of knowledge, with which I have been largely concerned, has a certain essential subjectivity; it asks how do I know what I know,' and starts inevitably from personal experience. The data are egocentric."[10]

Could anyone deny that this individualism, this egocentric approach, was an inevitable aspect of the general individualism of rising bourgeois thought? Just this alone would be enough to convert knowledge into an insoluble problem. One of Descartes' contemporaries, indeed, had a brilliant insight into this question. Descartes had argued that the ideas of perfection, of infinity, etc., that were involved in his concept of God could not have come from himself, a finite, imperfect being. The materialist theologian (the contradiction was a real one) Gassendi replied:

Nothing is more true than that they have not proceeded from you alone, so that you have had no knowledge of them derived from yourself and merely by means of your own efforts; for they have proceeded and are derived from objects, from parents, from masters, from teachers, and from the society in which you have moved. But you will say: 'I am mind alone: I admit nothing outside of myself, not even the ears by which I hear nor the people who converse with me.' You may assert this: but would you assert it, unless you heard us with your ears, and there were men from whom you learned words? Let us talk in earnest, and tell me sincerely: do you not derive those word-sounds which you utter in speaking of God, from the society in which you have lived? And since the sounds you use are due to intercourse with other men, is it not from the same source that you derive the notions underlying and designated by those sounds? Hence though not due to you alone, they do not seem on that account to proceed from God, but to come from some other quarter.[11]

This extraordinary anticipation of the Marxist approach has been overlooked and ignored. It recognized the social nature of knowledge. It exposed the hollowness and limitations of the approach not only of Descartes but of Locke too. They could not see knowledge as something that arises and exists only in society, only in the necessity of production and intercourse. Locke says he is going to inquire into the origins, certainty, and extent of human knowledge, but then he proceeds to take as the origin, not the development of knowledge over the ages of mankind's primitive life and the rise of civilization, but its "origin" in his own head precisely as if he had been born a Robinson Crusoe on a desert island.

He confuses knowledge theory with "individual" psychology, and does not understand that human consciousness is "from the very beginning a social product, and remains so as long as men exist at all."[12]

This ignoring of the social nature of knowledge appears further in the notion that one knows oneself before and more than all else. Descartes and Locke both know "themselves" and the sensations and ideas in their own minds before they know anyone or anything else. Each "proves" that he exists, then that God exists, and then they turn to the question of the existence of everything else and their knowledge of it. Locke even entitles the key chapter of his work, "Our Knowledge of the Existence of Other Things," meaning by "other things," everything besides himself and God. Here, again, the Epicurean Gassendi of the seventeenth century was on the right track. He wrote to Descartes:

But here it occurs to me to wonder how you can be said to have an idea of yourself (and one so fertile as to furnish you with such a supply of other ideas) . . .; when, nevertheless, you have really either no idea of yourself, or one which is very confused and imperfect. . . . What if it be the case that, as you do not and cannot possess an idea of yourself, it may be said that anything else is more capable of being easily and clearly perceived by you than yourself.[13]

Most interestingly, Gassendi continues by arguing that one knows himself only as the eye sees itself, that is, in a mirror, and that without this there is no hope of knowing yourself. He does not say, however, what this mirror is, though he may have had an idea of it. Marx understood the nature of this mirror and that it consisted of other people. He wrote in *Capital*:

In a sort of way, it is with man as with commodities. Since he comes into the world neither with a looking glass in his hand, nor as a Fichtean philosopher, to whom "I am" is sufficient, man first sees and recognizes himself in other men. Peter only establishes his own identity as a man by first comparing himself with Paul as being of like kind.[14]

Both Descartes and Locke, like virtually all classic philosophers, took for granted that we know ourselves first and then know other things. Locke made the additional error of thinking that we know *sensations* first and the things of the world second. He further believed that we know sensations better than we know things. But in experience we have direct relationship with the things around us. Only subsequently do we discover *sensations* as a phase of the total process of experiencing things.

The failure to see the social origin and nature of knowledge was the first basic error in virtually the whole classic approach to knowledge theory. Not to see knowledge socially was also not to see it historically, and when it is not viewed from the standpoint of history it is certain to be analyzed in static and metaphysical terms. As Lenin said, theory of knowledge must too "regard its subject matter historically, studying and generalizing the origin and development of knowledge, the transition from non-knowledge to knowledge."[15]

The second error is that of seeing knowledge only in terms of contemplation. Locke and Descartes, even though they have, theoretically, a practical approach to knowledge, as has been seen, never were able, practically, to connect knowledge with the labor process. Mankind, or mind, stands on one side, nature, the world, on the other. They so separated the two that they never could get them together. Theory and practice have no real linkage. Knowledge is looked at less as a necessity for mankind's daily life, and inseparable from it, than as a luxury which we might or might not be able to obtain. They are, as it were, visitors in the universe. And they ask whether they have or have not the equipment necessary to know it. Their very approach dooms them from the start. Locke wrote an almost incredible passage, after chapters of increasing difficulty in getting back from our sensations and ideas to their external causes, in getting from mind to matter, from ideas to that which they reflect. He insists that we can know nothing but what is actually before our senses—he speaks of such a collection of sensations "as is wont to be called man"—which means that we can know nothing really of the past, the future, or anything we are not now seeing, hearing, tasting or smelling. He concludes that such reliance on our senses *"may procure us convenience, not science"* and he is led to suspect that there can be no *science* of nature.[16] Practice is thus separated from theory, "convenience" from "science." Here is the true origin of pragmatism—the whole of Dewey's philosophy is the elevation of Locke's difficulty and dilemma into the principle that all the categories of our thought and conclusions of the sciences are but convenient "instruments" for organizing future experience rather than constituting knowledge of the world around us.

No other conclusion is possible once "mind" is taken out of its social-historical context—out of the process whereby human beings organize their relations to one another and to nature to produce the necessities of their lives—and converted into a *spectator* of a universe essentially foreign to us. But this is the dilemma of all classical philosophy. Diderot almost found his way out. Hegel seemed to escape it and to establish our knowledge as real knowledge of the real world. He did this, however, only idealistically, only by making the external world a product of mind or spirit in the first place. Thus he did not solve the problem but only got out of the bag what he had first put in it.

Descartes and Locke remain in theory what they were in fact, observers of the world and not participants in changing it through the process of labor. The difference between them is that Locke, not satisfied with abstract thinking, as Marx said of Feuerbach, appeals to *"sensuous contemplation,"* but he cannot conceive sensation, the experience of our senses, as a form of practical human activity.

After Locke came the deluge. What for Locke were *difficulties* in his desire to prove that we have knowledge of the real world, became for his successors *opportunities* for denying the possibility of real knowledge. Something of the story of Berkeley and Hume has already been told in the preceding chapter. Not having Locke's bourgeois revolutionary purpose, they sought only to hold back any further progress and any further revolutionary change. With them, knowledge becomes not an expression of our relationship with the world outside us, but a veil between us and any objective reality. That which arose through the ages of mankind's labors in maintaining its life, becomes a screen on which a world is painted either by God as with Berkeley or by habit or "animal faith" as with the Humeans. And it matters little if we take the painting on the screen as the only reality or as the only reality we can know. In neither case do we know the nature of things, in neither case is our knowledge the reflection of the objective real world.

The French materialists of the eighteenth century never even tried to solve the knowledge problem that had been dumped into their laps. Most of them, indeed, never recognized that there was a problem on their hands. They blithely took over Locke's "empiricism" and went on, guided by their revolutionary purpose, to construct a materialist world outlook. For them Locke had established the one necessary thing, had laid the indispensable foundation. Never before, in the ancient or earlier modern world, had the materialist thesis that knowledge comes only through our senses, and that without sensation there can be no ideas in our minds, been so firmly and convincingly established. So they let it go at that, with the exception of the greatest mind among them. Denis Diderot alone recognized that there was a discrepancy between Locke's sensations and the whole materialist world view. How is it, he asked, that Berkeley and Hume can derive their idealism from the very knowledge theory from which the French materialists sought to derive their materialism?[17] He thought someone ought to investigate this question and ascertain where the ways parted, but he never attempted to do it himself. Even Diderot could not possibly have seen the thorough-going revolution in philosophy that would have to take place before the question could be solved. For the solution of the *problem* of knowledge that class society had raised, had itself become, with the advent of the industrial working class, a *practical* question, and not merely a theoretical one.

Something of the story of Humeanism and its development down to the present day has been discussed in the preceding chapter. It is necessary here to deal only with certain aspects of the knowledge question. The basic element of the Humean —read Machian, positivist, pragmatist, etc.—method is simple, in spite of its ramified and often disguised variations. It is that in all knowing we know not that which exists outside our knowledge, something of which our sensations and ideas are the reflection, but only our ideas themselves. The discoveries of the scientist are, as the *New York Times* editorializes, not discoveries at all, but inventions. They are so many devices, instruments, etc., invented by scientists to simplify the organization of their experience. "After all," the *Times* declares, "a revolutionary theory of gravitation or of the structure of the Universe is not a statement of truth, but an invention conceived to explain what is observed or experienced. Like any machine a theory must work."[18]

Such is the wisdom of the apologists of imperialism. No longer able to master the world, they deny that it has any existence outside of their minds. And this comes precisely at the time when science has made such colossal strides forward—strides represented most dramatically by the development of atomic energy, the release of the energy in the nucleus of the atom. One philosopher of science, indeed, Professor Philip Frank of Harvard University, was reported as saying, after the first explosions of atom bombs, that now "it had been shown that matter can disappear from the world, that the mass can be converted into energy."[19]

This is the position with which the college and university students are being indoctrinated today. It is the new, atomic-age opium of the intellectuals. The reason that it pervades philosophy and science, as it does, is to be found less in philosophy and science than in politics and economics. It is the best instrument the bourgeois intelligentsia have been able to discover for beating Marxism. It is old-fashioned to believe in an objective reality and in causality. Marxists are consequently dogmatists, hang-overs of the confidence of scientists in the nineteenth century that they were really learning something about the nature of things.

It is not required here to deal in detail with the various forms of contemporary positivism. Lenin's *Materialism and Empirio-Criticism* developed the techniques for uncovering Humeanism in whatever dress it chooses to masquerade, exposed its reactionary character and its service to religion, and provided a genuinely materialist approach to knowledge. Cornforth, in his two books on the subject, *Science and Idealism* and *In Defense of Philosophy*, has explored the most important forms Humeanism has taken since Lenin wrote. It is sufficient here to get a general picture of the position and of the answer to it that Marxism alone provides.

The following four quotations contain the kernel of contemporary Humeanism:

(1) I don't really believe in astronomy except as a complicated description of part of the course of human and possibly animal sensation. (F. P. Ramsey.)[20]

(2) That the sun will rise tomorrow, is an hypothesis; and that means that we do not *know* whether it will rise. A necessity for one thing to happen because another has happened does not exist. There is only *logical* necessity. At the basis of the whole modern view of the world lies the illusion that the so-called laws of nature are the explanations of natural phenomena. (L. Wittgenstein.)[21]

(3) Why . . . when a number of people see the sun should we believe that there is a sun outside their percepts, and not merely that there are laws determining the circumstances in which we shall have the experience called "seeing the sun?" (Bertrand Russell.)[22]

(4) Pragmatic philosophers did not invent the idea of the nature of the scientific object here put forth. . . . Duhem, for example, many years ago presented a view which amounted in effect to saying that scientific objects are symbolic devices for connecting together the things of ordinary experience. Others have held that they were devices for facilitating and directing predictions. (John Dewey.)[23]

Innumerable similar passages could be garnered from these **and many other philosophers** of our time. These are not exceptional but typical, and represent the dominant trend in Western Europe and America in the twentieth century. The first passage follows the incredibly cynical and contemptuous dismissal of philosophy as having to do with "beliefs" about the world quoted earlier. Ramsey here frankly states his belief that the sciences reveal to us nothing concerning the nature of things but are only complicated ways of putting together our sensations. Why he brings animals into the picture is a mystery. If planets and stars are only sensations, why should animals be thought to exist outside of me? If I don't know the sun exists and the earth goes around it, how can I possibly know that animals exist, much less that they have sensations? Let us leave till later the question of the existence of other people. To sum up, the sciences in this view are simply ways of linking together or "describing" our sensations.

The second passage is equally representative and revealing. From Wittgenstein to his disciple Russell, as from Dewey to his disciples Sidney Hook and James Burnham, the question of the sun's rising tomorrow is completely hypothetical. It is quite natural that this should be the case, since the question of there being a sun at all is equally hypothetical. This problem of the sun's rising has bothered the philosophers considerably. If it is not inevitable that the sun will rise tomorrow, if it does not rise of necessity because of the earth's rotation on its axis, then clearly socialism is not inevitable and nothing happens of necessity in the social world. This is indeed a boon for an imperialism plunging dizzily towards its destruction. "Anything can happen," the Humeans teach, but since nothing *must* happen, maybe the present system can continue indefinitely—miracles may yet save it, as the historian Arnold Toynbee teaches.

Basic in the philosophy of Hume and all his disciples is the denial that there is any necessity in the world, any causality of such a nature that given one event or groups of events, something else necessarily follows therefrom. The doctrine of causality is age-old, inseparable from the rise of a scientific materialist viewpoint and indispensable for its development. Without causality there is no real knowledge of the nature of things. According to the Humeans pellagra is not caused by an inadequate diet, crises are not inherent in the very nature of capitalism, pressing the button does not *make* the light go on. If we find these things related in our experience it is simply an interesting fact, not a law of the interconnections of things. Such is the meaning of Wittgenstein's concluding sentence. Everything we mean by a scientific or materialist world-view depends on the recognition that there are laws or principles governing the movement of matter. This is what Wittgenstein calls an "illusion." If this is an illusion, then there is no recourse but the return to any and every form of ancient mythology or superstition. Few things could better show the absolute degradation of bourgeois philosophy in the twentieth century.

Bertrand Russell, who functions as a sort of "playboy" of classic philosophy, has the audacity to ask why we should think there *is* a sun when we see it. Why bother, he says in effect, to assume anything so unnecessary and superfluous as that there is a sun there. It is so much more reasonable, so much more "economical" just to have the sensation of the sun and let it go at that. That he should speak of "laws" governing the circumstances in which we have the experience we call "seeing the sun" is slightly fantastic, inasmuch as he doesn't believe in laws at all. But the reference is significant, nonetheless. It simply means that Russell doesn't object too much to mental, spiritual, psychological laws. It is only material, physical laws that are bad.

John Dewey is harder to quote in this context than are so many of his contemporaries because he seldom troubles to say exactly what he means. Passage upon passage is so vague and confused as to convey his real philosophy only to the initiated, while progressive-sounding statements demagogically mislead the non-professional in philosophy. In a statement written to answer some critics who questioned whether Dewey's philosophy did not do away with an objective world, he remains extraordinarily vague and indefinite. Look, he says, I am not doing anything so different or new. Did not Duhem (a French philosopher of the early part of the century who was in the Machian school and who was criticized by Lenin) say that scientific objects are simply "symbolic devices for connecting together the things of ordinary experience?" By scientific objects Dewey means any conclusions of scientific investigation, such as the proposition that the sun is 93,000,000 miles from the earth, 800,-000 miles in diameter, of such and such a surface temperature, etc., or that all the matter we know is composed of atoms of definite components and patterns. He is saying, therefore, that Duhem regarded all that science has or ever can find out concerning the phenomena of nature as simply convenient ways of connecting one experience with another. A simple illustration would be the teaching that the earth rotates every 24 hours on its axis. For Duhem and Dewey this proposition does not tell us anything real about an "earth," which, of course, is in turn a scientific object, since we do not see a globe with a circumference of 25,000 miles, etc. The proposition that the earth rotates on its axis is a "symbolic device" for linking together my experience of seeing the sun in the east, seeing it overhead, seeing it in the west, the stars coming up, and so forth. In other words, we don't see the sun in the east and then ever farther towards the west till it sets, because the earth turns on its axis. We merely make up the theory, the device of the earth's rotating, in order to link together the various places in which we seem to see the sun.

Could there be a more abject denial of all that mankind has learned about the world over hundreds of thousands of years? Dewey was the most controversial of all our contemporaries because he would never forthrightly state his true position. He has camouflaged his views more cleverly than any other. The sentence following those quoted, for example, reads: "Now my view does not go as far as these." And yet he never, in all that follows, explains how his view does not go as far as Duhem's or others, or just how far it does go. As mentioned earlier, when Dewey was questioned by the late Morris R. Cohen as to whether in his philosophy the earth existed prior to man, Dewey, instead of answering, criticized Cohen for asking such an old-fashioned question, and he offered the question as proof that Cohen simply had not and could not understand his philosophy or he would not have asked it.[24] Again, when Professor Arthur E. Murphy asked Dewey if the sun exists prior to our seeing it, Dewey indignantly refused to answer until he finally took refuge in answering another question altogether.[25] His position nevertheless, is clear to those who want to understand it, especially if they are forearmed with Lenin's *Materialism and Empirio-Criticism*.

But still the question troubles people: Why do the philosophers do this? The non-professional in philosophy generally finds it more difficult to understand why they would want to deny knowledge of the real world than to understand the method they have used to do it. In answering this question let us recall why the early modern philosophers, from Bruno and Bacon to Descartes and Locke, tended towards materialism and a scientific world view. They recognized the need of science for the development of productivity. Further, they required something of a scientific materialist outlook to combat the ideology of the feudal church and its landlords, and to advance that of their own class.

But what are the problems of the bourgeois class today? Intense contradictions center in the forces of production and their further development. They are over-developed in terms of the ability of the most advanced capitalist countries to utilize them profitably for peace-time purposes. But the challenge of the socialist section of the world provides the excuse for huge military expenditures and the necessity for increased productivity for world economic competition. These contradictions are made more acute by the discovery of atomic power and the development of automatic machinery.

On the one hand is the fear of a crisis of over-production and the resultant fear and distrust of science, such as was expressed in the depression years in a proposed "moratorium on science." On the other is the rapidly growing recognition that the United States is falling seriously behind the Soviet Union in the training of scientists, engineers and technicians in every field. Thus, within the same decade we have completely contradictory approaches to science. One leading scientist, Edmund W. Sinnott of Yale University, told the American Association for the Advancement of Science, upon his inauguration as President of that body in 1947: "Science is not the benefactor but the scourge of mankind."[26] And we recall again the statement of General Bradley that "We have too many men of science and too few men of God." Today public officials and the press discuss our backwardness in scientific education and the need for vast efforts to catch up with the Soviet Union.

The contradiction is a real one and it extends beyond the spheres of economic production and war preparation into those of social theory, philosophy and ideology generally. The bourgeoisie in the seventeenth and eighteenth centuries was fighting an outworn and reactionary feudal ideology. Science was a prime weapon in this struggle. Today the bourgeoisie is fighting a rising and progressive socialist world-outlook that is bidding against it for the minds of men. This philosophy challenges all illusions, all mythology, all irrational prejudices in the name of scientific materialism. Opposition to it, therefore, necessarily takes on a retrograde and anti-scientific character. Science is needed for economic competition and war. But its sting must be removed. Its ability to challenge the prevailing bourgeois mythology, with its idealist and religious roots, must be destroyed.

Professor Philipp Frank reveals one aspect of the motivation of the whole twentieth century resort to Humeanism in knowledge theory. The great contribution of Mach, he asserts, lay in his saving physics from its enemies. But who might its enemies be? Obviously none other than religion and the church, from which Mach "saved" physics by denying that it is knowledge of objective reality. Frank's meaning becomes clearer in another passage in the same book where he discusses Galileo and the Inquisition:

> What the Inquisition actually wanted of Galileo was only that he confess that the doctrine of the motion of the earth was correct merely as a mathematical fiction, but was false as a "philosophical" doctrine. We can also find in the standpoint of the Inquisition something corresponding to the modern relativistic conception. According to the latter, we cannot say that 'in reality' the earth moves and the sun stands still, but only that the description of phenomena turns out to be simpler in a coordinate system in which this is the case.[27]

This means nothing else than that if Galileo had not been so unenlightened, if he had only the understanding of the contemporary positivists and pragmatists, he would never have gotten into trouble with the Inquisition. True, they were dogmatic and believed that the earth stood still. But Galileo was equally dogmatic and believed it moved around the sun. He fell into their trap in believing that we could possibly know the real world, and thus went down before their might. Professor Frank is saying that the smart scientist today could never possibly get into such trouble, because he knows his science exists only in his head and refers to nothing objective and real. Thus, as

Lenin pointed out, the fashionable professors surrender to clericalism and reaction.

But one final thing must be noted. The scientists from Jeans
and Eddington, to Millikan, Sinnott, and the officers of the Rockefeller Foundation, are fundamentally far less concerned with
preserving religion than with preserving capitalism and what is
for them a comfortable *status quo.* In saving science from its
enemies they are not saving it for the church, but for the state,
for the rule of the bourgeoisie in a bourgeois world. Let them
waver in this and they are outcasts, are refused passports to go
abroad for scientific purposes, are denied all facilities for research. The history of positivism and pragmatism is less the
history of the development of man's knowledge of the surrounding world than it is the history of class struggles. And this was
true equally of the persecution of Bruno and Galileo. It was
not a question of an abstract battle between two theoretical approaches to questions, those of science and religion, but it was
a war between two social systems and the classes that represented
them. It is significant too that the great home of Machism and
logical positivism was in Vienna, a stronghold of clerical reaction and of reformist Social-Democracy. Here scientists really
did need to defend themselves against the church. But instead
of defending science against superstition, they surrendered to
superstition sole jurisdiction over the real, objective world—
leaving to science to know only the creations of our own imagi-
nations.

What is the answer of dialectical and historical materialism
to this betrayal of science and knowledge? How do Marxists
refute the positivist position and argument? This is a more subtle
problem than first meets the eye. Diderot, speaking of Berkeley,
commented that this idealism was the most absurd system the
mind had ever conceived "and the most difficult to refute." It
is, in the first place, most "economical." It needs to assume no
cause for our sensations and experience generally. It needs to
assume absolutely nothing outside our own heads. But already
a great difficulty presents itself, and one which pragmatism and
positivism, all of Humeanism, most carefully seeks to conceal
and cover up. There are only two alternatives here, although
Bertrand Russell succeeds in making many more.[28] Either *I*
know—and this problem cannot be escaped by the editorial

"we"—that other persons exist, or I don't. And here is the dilemma. From Berkeley and Hume to Russell and Dewey it has been utterly impossible for this school to prove that other people existed, and equally impossible to deny it. Russell comes nearer than most to expressing a desire to deny that anyone else exists, but then he proclaims his fear that in the majority of people, "human affections are stronger than the desire for logical economy," and that they will therefore not share his desire "to render solipsism [the doctrine that he alone exists] scientifically satisfactory." For the positivists, the existence of other people has become the bargain found in "Alice in Wonderland": "You believe in me and I'll believe in you."

Ramsey, as seen earlier, talked of the description of the course of human and animal sensation. But what right does he have to assume that astronomy is a description of the course of *human* sensation. By the principles of the whole Berkeleyan-Humean tradition—principles always ignored when it comes to this question of the existence of other people—he has no more right to talk of other people than he has to talk of other things. He denies that his sense data assure him that the sun and the stars exist, but then he admits that they give him knowledge of the existence of other people. But *I*, by their principles, have not a whit more evidence for assuming that *you* exist than I have for assuming the same concerning the ocean, the moon, China (of which I have never had any sensations) nor the previous existence of Copernicus or Galileo.

This is an impossible predicament and the less spoken of it in polite society the better the positivists like it. Bertrand Russell says, in effect, I would like to be a solipsist, but I cannot because some of my best friends are people. That is not, however, too different from the case of the American psychologist and logician of Columbia University, Professor Christine Ladd Franklin, who wrote, some years back, that she was a solipsist and was surprised that there were no others.

You can believe in objective reality—a reality beyond your sense experience and the cause of it—or not. But you cannot admit the existence of other people, including your mother or father, husband or wife, and deny objective reality. The only possible justification that could be advanced for this distinction is that in assuming other people, you are only assuming that mind or spirit exists, for of such is the essence of "people," while in assuming other *things* to exist, you are assuming matter. But this distinction will not work. For when it comes to the question of our knowledge, the question is not what does exist, but how do we *know* anything exists. By confusing the two questions, the Humeans evade responsibility, and smuggle other people into a world the very existence of which they vociferously deny. Solipsism is the skeleton in the closet of all subjective idealism, and few things embarrass its current disciples more than the exposure of their illogicality in refusing to accept it. For them to accept it is to commit suicide, and that is something no ruling class or its ideologists care to do.

There should be no confusion here between the knowledge question and the priority of thinking or being. One can believe if he wants to, that only spirit exists. On this basis one could justify believing that other people or minds exist but nothing material does. But the question at issue is not what one cares to believe, but what one can justify believing by a theory of knowledge. And by Humean principles and those of all his followers, there is no basis whatsoever for any one of them to believe that any other one of them exists. Santayana solves the problem with "animal faith" and that is what Russell did, in effect, in his major philosophical work, *Human Knowledge.* When human beings have to justify their knowledge of, and belief in, anything existing outside their individual heads by "animal instinct" or "animal faith," mankind has reached an extraordinarily low level. But fortunately, this is not a reflection on the human race, but on the ideologists of imperialism.

It has already been said that in terms of pure logic, Humeanism cannot be refuted. But it can be logically reduced to the absurd and unpalatable extreme of solipsism. The real refutation is found in practice—in the whole of human production and creative activity. When attention is turned to practice, Humeanism and all its contemporary expressions vanish into thin air. Hume himself was forced to admit this. In one memorable passage, he wrote:

Most fortunately it happens, that since reason is incapable of dispelling these clouds [of scepticism] nature herself suffices to that purpose, and cures me of this philosophical melancholy and delirium, either by relaxing this bent of mind, or by some avocation and lively impression of my senses, which obliterates all these chimeras. I dine, I play a game of Backgammon,

I converse, and am merry with my friends: and when after three or four hours amusement, I would return to these speculations, they appear so cold, and strained, and ridiculous, that I cannot find in my heart to enter into them any farther.[29]

This has generally been regarded as a charming passage, and one could certainly suspect that it was written for the very purpose of charming and disarming its readers. But from any healthy viewpoint it is more corrupt than charming. It is an unusual testimony to the degradation that ensues upon the separation of theory and practice. Though it was for his opposition to democracy that Jefferson called Hume "this degenerate son of science," it applies to his philosophy as well.

The Gospel according to St. John opens with the sentence, "In the Beginning was the Word." Goethe opposed to this the assertion, "In the Beginning was the Deed." The difference is a big one. It expresses the question: Which comes first, theory or practice? And though much has been written on this question, from the Hippocratic physicians to Paracelsus, Vesalius, Leonardo, and Francis Bacon, not until the rise of class consciousness in the modern working-class and its subsequent philosophical expression in Marxism, did there develop a clear-cut and scientific approach to the question of the relation of theory and practice.

The basis for this has already been discussed in Chapter II on the working-class challenge. Applied to knowledge theory it means simply this: Knowledge arises out of practice, based in the first instance on needs and interests which *must* be satisfied if the race is to survive. And its test, the standard for determining its correctness and adequacy, is, again, human practice. As Engels put it, simply and eloquently, in his discussion of this very Humean position: though the argumentation is hard to beat, "before there was argumentation, there was action. And human action had solved the difficulty long before human ingenuity invented it." And he continued:

The proof of the pudding is in the eating. From the moment we turn to our own use these objects, according to the qualities we perceive in them, we put to an infallible test the correctness or otherwise of our sense perceptions. If these perceptions have been wrong, then our estimate of the use to which an object can be turned must also be wrong, and our attempt must fail. But if we succeed in accomplishing our aim, if we find that the object does agree with our idea of it, and does answer the purpose we intended it for, then that is positive proof that our perceptions of it and of its qualities, so far, agree with reality outside ourselves. . . . So long as we take care to train and to use our senses properly, and to keep our action within the limits prescribed by perceptions properly made and properly used, so long we shall find that the results of our action prove the conformity of our perceptions with the objective nature of the things perceived. Not in one single instance, so far, have we been led to the conclusion that our sense perceptions, scientifically controlled, induce in our minds ideas respecting the outer world that are, by their very nature, at variance with reality, or that there is an inherent incompatibility between the outer world and our sense perceptions of it.[30]

What Engels is pointing out here is more far-reaching and revolutionary than first meets the eye. Unlike Dewey, who makes a great show of being "practical" and of making practice the test of knowledge, Engels is saying that practice *has* tested our knowledge and constantly is testing it. For Dewey, practice only *will* "test" our knowledge. The distinction has often been overlooked, deliberately by Sidney Hook and others who wished to show that Dewey's instrumentalism was simply Marxism brought up to date; mistakenly by liberal socialists who have failed to see the distinctions between practice as a social-historical criterion and practice as consisting solely of experiments *to be performed in the future*. For Marx and Engels we have learned, are learning, and will learn as our experience expands and our practice extends into ever new realms. For Dewey we are *about to learn* in the future, but never have learned in the past, and cannot in the present. Dewey's pretended unity of theory and practice is completely fraudulent. It is not really about practice or experiments at all that he is speaking, but the organization of our *experience* in the future. This allows him forever to talk about practice but never to learn from it. Hume had to confess the complete irreconcilability of theory and practice in his thought. Dewey covers it up by relegating their unity to the future.

It is only the modern industrial working class that can solve this problem. The reason is simple. For workers, the table is not a collection of sensations in somebody's mind, but a product of labor. The present writer not long ago heard two Columbia University students prove to each other's perfect satisfaction on a subway train between 116th Street and Times Square, that it was perfectly ridiculous for anyone to think that anything existed outside of anyone's sensations. But workers know better because they *built* the subway with their labor and sweat, and run the trains to boot. For the whole Humean tradition a Constellation roaring overhead is an interesting collection of sense data which comes from they know not what. But the workers of the Lockheed corporation know what it comes from—they made it.

The very development of technology and industry has made the whole question ever more fictitious. For people do not live in a world of sense impression gathered from they know not what. Neither do they live in a world that is just *given* to them by they know not whom. An old American story illustrates this delightfully. It tells of a city clergyman who, travelling in the country, stops at a crossroad and converses with a farmer who is resting on his plough for a moment at the end of a furrow. The clergyman surveys the fields and remarks: "What a beautiful farm God has given you," to which the farmer replies, "Yes, but you should have seen it when he had it alone."

The moral is that the fields we work in, the cities we live in, the whole of our surroundings, are no longer natural, but manmade. We have changed the face of the earth by our labor, and consequently have determined the sensations we do and will receive, the experience of the world we have. Even our trees are not what they were before we intervened. They are neither of the same kind in many cases, and more rarely are they in the same place. The eucalyptus of California that so characterizes the landscape in many sections, was brought there a few generations ago from Australia. The fruit trees we admire are the product of age-old cultivation, crossing, grafting, and the like. Even the animals we surround ourselves with, the dogs and horses, the cows and chickens, are a product of human creative activity in making nature over to suit our purposes. Our knowledge is embodied in the things we make, in hybrid corn and seedless oranges, in houses, radios, and electric lights. This is the refutation of Humeanism in all its forms. We not only know the world but change it, and the very world we know is itself a product of the work of our ancestors. Against this simple fact, the attempts of those who wish to deny that we can know anything outside our heads rings hollow and appears to be what it

is—a miserable and pathetic apology for the existing order and
an attempt to stem the tide of progress.

The relation of knowledge and practice appears here with
perfect clarity. Changing the world, practice, requires knowledge if it is to fulfill objectively realizable purposes, while that
very process of changing the world is in itself the surest path
to new knowledge. Nothing can be truly and fully known without relation to some possible use we can put it to, and equally
nothing can be effectively used without the acquisition of new
knowledge of its properties and relationships. The great American plant-breeder, Luther Burbank, beautifully expressed this
distinction between knowledge integrated with practice and con-
templative passive knowing. After reading Darwin's "Animals
and Plants Under Domestication," published in 1868, Burbank
wrote his life's dedication: "I desired to deal with the forces of
life, and to mold the plastic forms of living organisms—rather
than to spend my life in classifying the fixed and immutable
phenomena of dead organism."[31]

Occasionally, a philosopher of the old school, that is, one who
has not decisively broken with the prevailing capitalist modes
of thought, seeks nevertheless to break through the nonsense
of pragmatism and positivism. Roy Wood Sellars, of the University of Michigan, is such a one. He has read Lenin and has
seen that Marxism alone, of all the philosophies of the past century, has punctured the myth of subjectivism and has stuck
steadily to its guns.[32] But when Sellars himself attempts to deal
with the question of knowledge, and seeks to answer such
Humeans as Bertrand Russell, he commits a significant and unhappy error. Correctly, Sellars shows that from Descartes to
Russell, philosophers have had engrained in them—he does not
dream of asking why—the notion that they ought to doubt the
perception of the things they practically see and do, even the
typewriter they are hammering. And Sellars *refutes* this with
"they know perfectly well that they bought the typewriter years
ago and it needs repair—or that they are turning over the good
earth with their spades, also bought."[33] Although this is not
bad, it is not good enough. One might call it the petty-bourgeois theory of knowledge, for its slogan is: "I bought it, therefore it exists," or in other words to be is to be a commodity.
Workers would approach the question differently. For them the

typewriter exists because they made it, and they have determined to use it too, just as they use the spades. For the worker and the farmer, there is no *problem* of knowledge, there is only the question of what we have learned thus far and what we yet need to know, the better to master nature and the conditions of our life.[34]

Behind the whole classic tradition is the notion that knowledge is a peculiar something that exists only in our heads. We have already shown the reasons for this illusion. But knowledge exists not only in the medium of our minds or brains, but is embodied in our tools, in all the things we make and all the things we make them with. It is embodied in our skills and habits, in that "know-how" that is indispensable for the continuation of human life for every day and every hour on this earth. Our knowledge of the stuff and laws of nature is crystallized and exhibited in every object surrounding us and everything we do. It is the illusion, peculiar to the intellectual divorced from the labor process, that knowledge exists only in our heads, or our books. On the contrary, knowledge is embodied in the clothes we wear and the food we eat, the houses we live in and the roads we travel on, and in the plants and animals we use for food. Every one of these testifies to our knowledge of nature, and together they indicate the immense strides we have made in gaining ever more accurate and more adequate truths concerning the nature of things. But, for reasons developed already in earlier chapters, it was left to the working class to attain these insights and to apply them to the revolutionizing of philosophy for the purpose of the revolutionizing of society.

The great leader of the Chinese revolution, Mao Tse-tung, in his essay already referred to on knowledge theory, has eloquently expressed this historic role of the working class. He wrote, in 1937:

At the present stage of the development of society the responsibility of correctly understanding the world and of changing it has already fallen with the whole weight of history upon the shoulders of the proletariat and its political party. This process of the practice of changing the world on the basis of a scientific knowledge of it has already reached a historic moment both in China and in the whole world, a moment of such importance as the world has never witnessed before. This change is none other than the complete overturn of the world of darkness both in China and elsewhere and its transformation into a world of light that never existed before.[35]

For working people there is no problem of knowledge. There is only the problem of the use of knowledge for the abolition of poverty in a world that can produce plenty, for the elimination of exploitation in a world where all can live in peace and happiness. But this brings us to the subject of values, of the goods people seek. It is no longer a question of whether we can know and what we do know. It is a question of what we want life in this world to be, and what we can make it into when unfettered by the trammels of class society. Knowledge is the prerequisite without which such revolutionizing of our world is impossible. But such change requires motivation, too, specific moral ideals and purposes. And towards these the working class is impelled by the conditions of its life.

Chapter V

TOWARDS A SCIENTIFIC
MATERIALIST ETHICS

It is of profound historic significance that it was left to the theorists of the working class to achieve an adequate and scientific theory of moral values that would transform and revolutionize all previous ethics. If the nature of exploiting society made impossible the solution of the problem of the relation of mind and matter, and prevented an understanding of the origin and nature of knowledge, how much less possible was it for the philosophers of class society to develop a scientific and all-human morality?

How could the thinkers of an exploiting class possibly be expected to be "objective" in their idea of a good life? The question "good for whom?" immediately arises and the answer must be, "good for us." For slave owners, and those who live and thrive on the slave system, the only "ideal" life is the life of "ideal" slave owners. So must it also be for feudal lords and capitalist merchants, industrialists, and bankers. When a class is progressive its ideas of the good, the good life and a good society, have progressive features. This is not because such a class is more "altruistic" than a preceding ruling class but because its needs and interests are wider and must embrace to some extent those of other classes. In concrete situations, this varies with the differing wings of one and the same class, as from the American revolution through to the triumph of Jeffersonianism. But no class interested in the perpetuation of class society with its accompanying maintenance of privilege for a few could possibly formulate an objective, scientific and all-human ethic. It could not wish to do so. It could not believe in the possibility of such a thing. Yet the reading of the history of ethical thought, from China to England and America, reveals precisely the claim to such impartiality. From the "Golden Rule"

to Kant's "categorical imperative," from "the meek shall inherit
the earth," to the blessings of the "free world" of the U.S. imperialists, the limited values of a minority of society are set up as
the highest and truest values of all mankind.

The idealist moralists failed to understand where moral values
come from. Furthermore, they made moral values so abstract
as to be meaningless as guides to conduct. They centered all
attention on the "goodness" of the individual and ignored the
needs of social life. They provided standards of personal conduct
and neglected the standards or criteria for evaluating social
institutions. And, among other things, they separated material
values from moral values, moral from aesthetic, and these from
religious or spiritual values, thus making separate "realms of
value" at the expense of any unified good of human life.

Spiritualists dominated moral thinking throughout the whole
history of class society. They first created a "problem" of value
and then proceeded to solve it through the separation of mind
and matter, body and soul—deriving all value from some higher,
non-material, spiritual principle. The materialists, generally
representing rising and progressive classes, opposed the idealists
and strove to establish an objective and down-to-earth ethics.
They made notable advances, but confined by class limitations
and the same metaphysical approach, they could not escape from
giving abstract and static answers to mankind's most concrete and
dynamic problems. Further, by the very nature of their mechanical materialist method, they found difficulty in moving from the
good of each individual, taken separately, to social wellbeing.

The parallel between the question of ethics or moral values
and that of knowledge is so close that many of the same difficulties of classic philosophy are found in both. Are moral judgments derived from God? Can we make moral judgments on any
objective grounds? Do and can they mean more than my individual subjective tastes? Are they derived from pure speculation or from the actual conditions of life? Do they refer to the
conditions of real people in the real world or to spiritual "first
principles," or psychological states?

One question has permeated the thinking of the philosophers
through the ages, from Plato to John Dewey: How could there
possibly be any values, any goods, in our judgments of things
and events, if they were not already contained in the non-human
world?

In other words, how can things and events be good or bad to us if they are not so "in themselves"; if the quality of goodness (or badness) is not inherent in them. It can readily be seen that either this approach, or one that reduces all values to pure subjective taste or preference, are the only idealist alternatives to the materialist teaching that goodness and all values are derived from human social existence.

Plato answered this question by putting all values in his eternal realm of ideas. Dewey answers it by denying that there is any world of nature outside our experience. Both, obviously, proceed from the assumption that man can have no values and make no meaningful moral judgments in a purely material world. In knowledge theory we find the exact parallel: a material world outside our minds could never be known by such philosophers, therefore, there either is no such objective world or it is not material.

Here, too, as in all other major philosophical questions, the classic mechanical materialists do battle against the idealists. They often fought most valiantly. They discovered important truths in their struggle, but the limitations of class society fell like a shadow on both sides alike. It stymied the materialists in this as it did in respect to knowledge. Just as they sought to prove that we can have knowledge of the world and that it comes through our senses, they sought in ethics to show that people can and do make moral judgments without benefit of God or clergy, and they make them somehow out of their life experience. But just as in knowledge theory they ignored practice, production, so in ethical theory they divorced themselves from the needs and interests of the masses of working people and from the whole historic process of the class struggle in relation to the development of mankind's forces of production. Finally, we will find that in certain questions of ethics, as in philosophy generally, the mechanical materialists opposed the idealists with such limitations of their own, that they played into the hands of their opponents. This is not to say that such pioneer thinkers as Epicurus and Helvetius were fighting a sham battle, but only that, however unwittingly, they confused important theoretical issues.

We shall examine first the mechanical materialist case against the idealists and then the working class or dialectical materialist criticism of the classic materialists.

All materialism has been subjected to vigorous attacks and continued misrepresentations since the fifth century B.C., but in no sphere of thought has the distortion gone to such lengths as in ethics. If it is grudgingly admitted that a materialist can have an ethics, such admission has usually been followed by the insistence that it is an ethics of the jungle, the barnyard, if not of the stock exchange. The very meaning that the term "Epicurean" has acquired, bears witness to the degree of distortion materialism has undergone at the hands of its enemies, while a favorite canard repeated monotonously from generation to generation is that materialists have no ideals, but are wholly taken up with the selfish and sodden pursuit of "material" things. The idealists have been aided in this attack on materialist ethics through the ambiguity in the word "idealism." As popularly used, idealism means belief in goals, standards or "ideals." Philosophically, it has nothing whatever to do with ideals but only with "ideas," and is simply the teaching that mind or spirit or *idea* is primary and matter secondary, subordinate, or indeed, completely non-existent. To have social and moral ideals has nothing to do, therefore, with philosophical idealism, any more than not to have any such ideas is connected with philosophical materialism. Only the greatest confusion results if this distinction of meaning is ignored.

Philosophical idealists have presented themselves as men of ideals *par excellence*. Organized religion has fostered these misconceptions for its own special theological and practical ends. Philosophical idealists have abetted them as an aid in proving their point against all forms of materialism and naturalism. There is evidence from both the ancient and modern worlds that entrenched ruling groups have encouraged such distortions, while in the contemporary world crisis they appear with increasing frequency and vehemence. Statesmen, journalists, and salaried writers of all descriptions vie with one another in allegations any student of the history of philosophy can readily disprove. Mr. Harold E. Stassen, for example, says: "The materialistic philosophy that man can live by reaching for bread alone is being proved in Russia a philosophy that fails to attain even the bread."[1] Similarly, Mr. Russell Porter, business analyst of the

New York Times, wrote of the "new ruling class in Russia" as having "based all its philosophy and its promises upon materialistic things and denied all moral and spiritual values. . . ."[2] Or again, Mr. Clement Attlee, in addressing a British Labor Party meeting, said that British socialism had never been a "materialist creed," and that "there never was a time when it was more necessary that work should be inspired by an ideal . . . our movement is not materialistic but is based on the acceptance of moral values. . . ."[3] In similar vein, Mr. John Foster Dulles holds: "The sovereignty of man rests upon a religious estimate of his nature. Without that estimate he tends to slavery."[4]

Anyone can multiply such statements for himself indefinitely. The common feature of them all is that materialism is alleged to involve the denial of all values, or at least of all but purely physical ones. Clare Booth Luce expressed this most clearly when she said that Communism, resting as it does on the denial of man's immortal soul, "that man is a child of God," necessarily opposes marriage and the family, denies objective truth, and reduces men to automata without individual rights of thought or action.[5] Such stupidities and misrepresentations would scarcely be worth citing in a serious study of ethics were it not that they express on a popular level the teachings of anti-materialist moralists from Plato to Kant and Dewey. And the materialist must add that on this popular political level they clearly reveal special pleading for ends and goals such as United States world domination, that cannot be justified by any honest presentation.

The fact is that materialism as a philosophy has had an ethics from ancient India and ancient Greece to the present day.[6] The real issue has been not its lack of ethical ideals but the kind of ideals it has. The issue has been not its ability to have an ethics but the material foundation of its moral values. The idealists did not like its ideals because they were centered in this world and man's life in it. They did not like the way it derived its ideals because it got them from the nature of human beings and not from the commands of a God or a so-called "moral law."

It will be seen later that this classic materialism left much unexplained and that its moral ideals offered only a "theoretical" challenge to existing society. But the idealists were not interested in correcting its defects. They were frightened lest any break in the fabric of traditional religious thought and idealist philosophy might bring the whole social structure crashing to the ground. History reveals that they were unduly alarmed, yet the fact remains that mechanical materialist ethics did eventuate, at its best, in the utopian socialism of St. Simon, Owen and Fourier. At its worst it becomes an apology for capitalism, but at least on the concrete grounds of its productivity, as in the work of the American materialist philosopher-economist, the late Karl Snyder.

For an ethics to rise that was to be a real challenge not only to existing society but to all class society whatsoever, a drastic revolutionary change in philosophy and ethical theory was required. This can be seen most readily through an examination first, of the basic premises required for any materialist ethics, and then through an exploration of the special and peculiar limitations imposed on ethics by mechanical materialism—a mode of thought as characteristic of class society as is idealism.

The first premise of any materialist ethics must be: *all ideas of right and wrong, justice and injustice, the good man and the good life, are human creations, made by men and reflecting their nature and the conditions of their life.* Any Marxist will recognize at once both the validity of this premise and its abstractness as thus stated. This, like the following premises, is deliberately put abstractly because that is the way it was conceived until the Marxist revolution in ethical thought. Nevertheless, this is clearly the precondition for any scientific approach to the question of values. They are made by people, and made by them not in virtue of some inner moral principle implanted by God or heaven-knows-what in their souls (Kant). And they are our creations, not eternal entities that exist completely independent of us (Plato).

It is easy to see that this materialist principle is the ethical counterpart of Xenophantes' statement in the sixth century B.C., that if horses and oxen had hands and could paint as men do, "horses would paint the form of the gods like horses and oxen like oxen. Each would represent them with bodies according to the forms of each." There is every reason to believe that such was, among other things, the meaning of Protagoras' much disputed statement, "Man is the measure of all things." It is also clearly expressed by Heracleitus' statement: "Men would not have known the name of justice if there were no injustice," and by Epicurus' account of justice as "something found expedient in mutual intercourse." This basic materialist doctrine stands as firmly today as it did 2500 years ago against any teaching that our moral ideas and ideals came from God, or any other non-human, non-material source. Men, it asserts, make their moral values, their ethics, out of the materials at hand as given them in their sense experience.

The second premise follows closely upon the first. It is the materialist answer to the question: What is it in man and his life that leads and impels him to make moral judgments and formulate ideas of the good? The answer is that *all ideas of the good arise from and express the needs, interests, and desires of human beings*. Spinoza stated this with utmost simplicity: "In no case do we strive for, wish for, long for, or desire anything, because we deem it to be good, but on the contrary we deem a thing to be good, because we strive for it, wish for it, long for it, or desire it."[7] This is to say that all our judgments of moral value, of good and evil, justice and injustice, freedom and servitude, progress and reaction, are a product of human hopes, wishes, desires. Applied to the idea of freedom, for example, this means that people do not desire freedom because it is in some abstract way good, but that they call freedom their ability to achieve the goods they desire. From this materialist view, a good no one wants is a contradiction in terms.

A good that no one wants is like a right that no one has, except that people demand rights they do not have while they are "given," by others, goods they do not want! As Abraham Lincoln said of slavery: "Consider, if you can, any *good* thing, that no man wants for himself." Yet the history of ethical theory is as replete with ideals that ought to be, as the history of society is with wants that are not fulfilled. But the people are seeing the sleight of hand by which spiritual goods they are supposed to want are substituted for the material things they do want, and are saying, as a Negro clergyman did recently, that in Africa the people had the land and the missionaries came in with the Bible, but now the people have the bible while the white men have the land. When a ruling class is forced into reaction because it can no longer develop and use the forces of production for

the general well being, it always begins to glorify "inner freedom," the "inner life of the spirit," and to take refuge in the
parentheses of one or another sort of ethical idealism.

This materialist principle is in direct opposition to all idealist ethical theories, whether they be based directly on a divine
command, an eternal Platonic "idea," or a Kantian "moral law
within us." In no way does it limit the range of men's strivings, or desires, except that they aim at some kind of satisfaction.
There is nothing in this approach to justify any assertion that
men desire only so-called material things, that men can or want
to live "by bread alone." Spinoza himself eloquently expressed
his own conception of the range of human values in a note in
his *Ethics*:

> Assuredly nothing forbids man to enjoy himself, save grim and gloomy
> superstition. . . . Therefore, to make use of what comes in our way, and
> to enjoy it as much as possible (not to the point of satiety, for that would
> not be enjoyment) is the part of the wise man. I say it is the part of a
> wise man to refresh and recreate himself with moderate and pleasant food
> and drink, and also with perfumes, with the soft beauty of growing plants,
> with dress, with music, with many sports, with theatres, and the like,
> such as every man may make use of without injury to his neighbor.[8]

Unfortunately, a most important question is left unanswered
by Spinoza's formulation. He has established that human desires
and wishes constitute the good, determine moral values. But he
has left unanswered the question as to what people's strivings,
wishes, desires, and under what conditions, constitute an objective good? By an objective good is meant a good that is more
than any individual's particular wishes and desires. For a good
to be objective, it must be good for you or me or a class or all
human beings regardless of what you or I or any of us at any one
time think or feel. It is obvious that Spinoza is not in the subjectivist tradition of David Hume or Bertrand Russell who reduce the good to personal feelings, to individual taste. He believes, in fact, that only when individual desires are rationally
ordered in relation to the desires of all other individuals can
their realization be truly satisfactory for the individual, and be
harmonious with those of other individuals

Here in Spinoza is typified the insolubility of the problem
of any form of all-human ethics from within class society. What

is good for General Motors is not necessarily good for the nation, any more than what was good for the Roman patricians was good for the plebeians. The solution of the difficulty requires the concept of class—not to cement class relationships on mankind forever, but to eliminate them. Spinoza, the progressive, indeed the radical bourgeois, made enormous contributions to both political democracy and materialist philosophy. He was fighting for the progressive Dutch bourgeoisie against the princely Orange family with its still feudal relations. His thought beautifully reveals the fact that no one, regardless of how brilliant or how bold, could solve the problem of a class approach to a real non-class world until the modern working class first placed this on man's social and moral agenda. Feudalists could readily perceive slave exploitation; the bourgeois could equally well perceive feudal exploitation, but no bourgeois, materialist or idealist, could or ever can perceive bourgeois exploitation.

All bourgeois materialists, from Spinoza to Helvetius and Diderot, share this belief that, in bourgeois society the desires of all individuals can be rationally and harmoniously organized. Either this is possible or it must be admitted that there is no good beyond each single person's desire. No materialist can follow the latter alternative, for it is a denial of any objective good, whatsoever, as the Humeans so well understand. Here, again, Marxism alone is able to provide an answer.

The third indispensable premise of materialist ethics is that *the good as the end or goal refers only to this world and the life of people in it.* This is inevitable by any materialist principles, inasmuch as according to these there is no other place in which people can be good or enjoy the good life. Whatever any materialist in history believed to be good had to be good for people on this earth and in this life. A materialist might believe that we should "eat, drink, and be merry, for tomorrow we may die," or he might agree with Epicurus that "we cannot lead a life of pleasure which is not also a life of prudence, honor, and justice. . . . For the virtues have grown into one with a pleasant life, and a pleasant life is inseparable from them."[9] He may also believe as Diderot did when he wrote: "To try to leave after us a little more light and comfort than there was before, to improve and increase the heritage we have received; it is to that we should apply ourselves. I add: to do as much good as possible, and to spare as much suffering as possible around us, to all our companions on the way."[10] In short, as broad or as narrow as any particular materialist's goods and ideas may be, they must be "this-worldly," must be capable of being enjoyed by living human beings.

It must be clear to everyone that this materialist principle was a very positive achievement against all forms of religion and idealist philosophy. It has been aptly said that materialists refuse all promissory notes on heaven in favor of the good things of the earth. But, unfortunately, the classic materialists could not define the values of this world and this life more concretely. For them to do so, would be to run dangerously close to admitting that their society could not permit the masses of people to attain the values they themselves held to be good. The idealists solved this problem easily by holding up "eternal" and other-worldly goods, a higher spiritual life, eternal blessedness, and the like, as the true goods of mankind. The materialists, in class society, were forced to deny these and yet at the same time to remain exceedingly vague as to what the goods of human life were.

A fourth premise, required by the very nature of materialist philosophy, and standing in sharpest opposition to its idealist opponents, is that *material needs or goods are basic and the precondition of all other goods whatsoever.* In opposition to the injunction, "Seek ye first the Kingdom of Heaven," materialists have persistently maintained that before people can seek anything else, they must seek and obtain food, clothing, and shelter. Before men can satisfy any so-called higher or spiritual needs, they must satisfy a host of basic material ones, and therefore materialists (with extraordinary perversity from the spiritualist point of view) insist on the *primacy* of such material needs. For the materialist this means only that men cannot be happy, cultured, noble or generous unless they eat or have eaten, unless the material prerequisites of life have been present. It is certainly true that people sometimes, in the very quest for these basic material needs, sacrifice them individually that their class may attain them collectively, or sacrifice in the present for the sake of a richer future. That fact, does not, however, change the principle before us—rather, it confirms it.

The materialist may well understand that men cannot live

by bread alone, but he must hold that without bread they cannot live or seek values of any kind. When an American college president attacked, during World War II, the "Freedom from Want" of Franklin D. Roosevelt on the ground that "We are not fighting this war for a pint of milk a day for everybody, but for values," he was using philosophical idealism to express the opposition of the imperialists to raising the standard of living for a large section of the earth's population.

Not until the development of modern working-class thought could it be fully recognized that production is the first and basic human value. It follows that the pre-condition for the fulfillment of all other human values is the increase of the productivity of labor, the expansion of the forces of production and their utilization for raising the living standards of all members of society—something possible only under socialism. As was seen earlier, the materialist premises of ethics imply socialism, but the classic materialists were never able, as representatives of exploiting classes, to draw the logical conclusions. Marxists alone could see that the development of the forces of production underlies all other social activities and is the basic and indispensable social value. This means that great cultures can flourish only on an adequate economic base, and that culture for the masses of people depends on the achievement, in a classless society, of a standard of living that can come only with a high and expanding rate of industrial production.

Before developing the positive features of the Marxist revolution in ethical thought, it would be well to examine two criticisms which dialectical and historical materialism make of the whole classic materialist tradition. These are (1) that its concept of the good was always abstract and hence unable to serve concretely as an instrument of social progress, and (2) that classic materialism was almost universally unable to escape from individualism and achieve a genuinely social point of view.

The first of these defects deprived most materialist teaching of any relevance to the actual problems of people. The second deprived it of both an adequate explanation of human social behavior and of a genuine, realizable social goal. Both these limitations are illustrated by the Greeks, Aristippus and Epicurus, and by the general body of French materialism of the eighteenth century. They lent not only plausibility but a certain real justification to the counter-attacks of the idealists. Few things illustrate better than these limitations the metaphysical method that classic materialism had in common with idealism and throw better light on the restraints imposed upon all pre-Marxist thought as a result of its being the thought of exploiting class society.

Hedonism, or the doctrine of pleasure as the highest good, represents the abstract tendency of the materialist doctrine of moral value. Looking for the good as that which all men seek, Aristippus found it in pleasure and Epicurus in *ataraxia* or the less positive but more comprehensive tranquility. But are pleasure or *ataraxia*, or any similar ends, adequately comprehensive expressions of the concrete goods of human life, or sufficient guides to behavior and social action in concrete situations? It is safe to say that they are woefully inadequate to the ideals of a fully rounded individual personality, as these ideals develop even within class society. It is even safer to say that they offer nothing to, and indeed are out of reach of, the overwhelming majority of toiling mankind.

Idealists from Plato to Kant, as well as those of our own day, have effectively and often correctly criticized the pleasure theory, but they did so only to substitute special "higher" values of their own. In Diderot and d'Holbach there is to be found a genuine broadening of the moral end away from pure hedonism, but these men were on the whole better than their theory. It can safely be said that it was left to Marx and Engels, for the first time from a materialist standpoint, to break out from the limitations of any pleasure or happiness theory. They saw that this was but a limited and abstract expression of the needs, hopes, and aspirations of the masses of mankind. Engels wrote in criticism of the ethics of the materialist Ludwig Feuerbach: "Only very exceptionally, and in no case to his and other people's profit, can an individual satisfy his urge towards happiness by preoccupation with himself. Rather it requires preoccupation with the outside world, means to satisfy his needs, that is to say means of subsistence, an individual of the opposite sex, books, conversation, argument, activities for use and working up."[11]

Engels does not deny here that people seek happiness. That is not the question at issue. The question is the twofold one: Is personal happiness the be-all and end-all of individual endeavor? And does "happiness" adequately represent the complex sum-total of human hopes, wishes, desires, aspirations?

In answer to the first question, Engels is saying that if an individual seeks only to be happy, he is likely doomed to disappointment. But something still more important is involved. Let us suppose that a person could be offered a state of perfectly blissful happiness all the rest of his natural life, through let us say, a brain operation that would render him completely cheerful but ever afterwards unable to accomplish any creative work or to engage in political and social struggles on the basis of his own judgment of the issues? Can anyone deny that such an offer would have its takers? But would anyone affirm that the class-conscious worker or the socially conscious member of other classes would accept? But the refusal of any people to accept such an offer refutes all teaching that people seek only pleasure, happiness, tranquility, or anything else one wants to name it, regardless of what it is pleasure in, or from what the happiness is derived. This is what Aristotle meant when he said that no one would choose to live all his life with the mind of a child no matter how pleasant it might be.[12] This brings us to the second question.

We can and must say that pleasure or even the less restricted term, happiness, is an abstraction from the concrete goods that people seek and whose quest and possession constitute the good life. The classic materialist, from this point of view, substituted for the rich and variegated and endless goods of human life—goods of which we in our limited historical and class position can have only an inkling—one special psychological concomitant, and then made that stand for all the things, actions, situations from which it is derived. There were of course reasons for this peculiar limitation. For one thing, it seemed to the materialists in the struggle against all forms of spiritualist "goods" that pleasure or happiness was the most immediate, direct, and "tangible" object of human desire. Furthermore, it was enjoyed immediately by the individual and was akin, on this level, to the sensations which were the basis of all knowledge. It is easy to see the direct parallel between pleasure or happiness as the good and Lockean "sensations" as giving immediate and direct knowledge of things.

For another thing, the authors of this theory were members

of a leisure class, in the first instance, in slave society, and although their particular relations to society may have been quite different from those of Plato, they were nevertheless representatives of a class which found the necessities of life supplied by the labor of others. They themselves needed only to enjoy them, and to entertain themselves as the isolated and independent individuals in society they in fact were.

The idealists suffered in other ways from the same social limitations. They took, however, the task of administering the society from which they derived their sustenance more seriously. As a result, for example, in spite of all the reactionary and mystical elements in Plato's and Aristotle's thought, in contrast with the hedonists they at least saw the ethical problem as one of the "best" ordering of human social life and not as that of the degrees of pleasure or freedom from pain of so many separate atomic individuals. But the opposition between these two schools, which extends from the Greeks to the present day in ruling-class philosophy, strikingly reveals once more how ethical conceptions, like all others, have been conditioned by class society.

The second great limitation is but another expression of the atomism manifested in the first. From the ancient Greeks to Helvetius it seemed to be an indispensable concomitant of materialism itself. It is the assumption that each individual can and must seek only his own good. Although the metaphysical materialists were forced to introduce some social principles, some factor making for social harmony, this is looked upon only as something either required for the success of the individual's quest, or as a regulative principle society *ought* to employ to ensure that the struggle of individual wills results in some degree of social cohesion. Anyone can recognize at once that this theory has played a very important role in the development of bourgeois thought. "Everyone must look out for himself"; "We are all in it for what we can get," and so on *ad nauseam,* are simply expressions of the classic materialist teaching, and are but the other side of the coin represented by idealist appeals to unselfishness, philanthropy, and broadmindedness. One is tempted to say, indeed, that in moral theory and attitudes class society has required materialism no less than idealism—one to appeal to the self-interest of members of the ruling class and the other to disguise the rapacity of class exploitation.[13]

The best answer pre-Marxist materialism was ever able to give to the question of social responsibility and the need for the harmonizing of the innumerable pushes and pulls of individual wills, each seeking only its own good, was that unless we each took others' pursuit of their self-interest seriously, we would not be able to achieve our own. In other words, if we do not treat others with a certain degree of care our own self-interest will be thwarted. It takes little acumen to see that this is the same as the so-called "Golden Rule," which goes back at least to Egypt in the second millenium B.C. But in both cases it is a purely individualist principle—"I will be rewarded or punished personally in the quest of my happiness as a result of my treatment of others." This is a woefully limited basis for a truly human society, and utterly inadequate to account for the actual facts of human behavior, especially those revealed in the struggles of oppressed classes and peoples. D'Holbach did try to get something better when he asked: "Is there one wicked individual who enjoys a pure, an unmixed, a real happiness?"[14] But this is better taken as an illustration of d'Holbach's own good will and warm feeling for people than as a solution of the problem. What he is saying is that one can't be really happy if he is antisocial, but the limitations of the term happiness have already been pointed out, and there is absolutely no way of verifying d'Holbach's proposition.

Aristotle, although he rejected the dialectical principles of Heracleitus and denied their applicability to reality, was nevertheless in some of his analyses, a masterful dialectician. Thus he was enabled to solve a problem to which the idealists gave false spiritualist answers and which the materialists ignored. The problem is that of selfishness versus unselfishness. Does the individual act only for himself or for something else? Aristotle correctly recognized that the problem was one of action which satisfies the "self" of the individual acting and which yet enables him to act for some broad human, scientific, or cultural good.

Aristotle recognized the ambiguity of the term "self" in any teaching of self-interest as well as of unselfishness. Like the materialists, he started with the doctrine that the individual can perform no act that does not in some way bring satisfaction to himself. But he saw that the real problem lay in the fact that what satisfies him depends on the nature of his "self"—how narrow or how broad it is, how much it embraces. When one says, as Aristotle in effect did, that the self is as broad or as narrow as the range of its interests, then any proposition concerning self-interest as the principle of all behavior becomes an empty phrase. The ethical problem is converted from one of the opposition of so-called selfishness and unselfishness to one of the breadth of the individual's interests and the means whereby these interests can be broadened to include an ever larger segment of human society and its values. When Aristotle says that some men should be encouraged to be as diligent as possible in the pursuit of their "self-interest" because the more they pursue it the better off all of us are, he is simply saying that a person can be interested in doing and promoting things that are good for others too. And when he adds, conversely, that other men should be discouraged from pursuing their self-interests because the more they satisfy themselves the worse off everybody else is, he is saying that some people's interests are inimical to those of their fellows.[15]

Aristotle unfortunately added to this otherwise profound analysis of self-interest the comment that those who should be deterred from pursuing what interests or satisfies them are the overwhelming majority. This is nothing but an expression of his class prejudices, and has precisely the same meaning as the pronouncement by Alexander Hamilton in the American Constitutional Convention in 1787 that "The people are turbulent and changing; they seldom judge or determine right." It is the same idea already seen in Plato that workers and farmers cannot be entrusted with defending the state. It is the question whether the virtue and intelligence needed to manage society inhere in the "classes" or the masses, and was beautifully answered by Jefferson when he wrote: "Educate and inform the whole mass of the people. . . . They are the only sure reliance for the preservation of our liberty."[16]

A genuinely dialectical approach to the question of "self-interest" is impossible for an exploiting class. Either they teach the most naked and unabashed self-seeking or give themselves up to the most vapid professions of the glories of unselfishness. Often enough they teach both at the same time. Unable to have a dialectical conception of self-interest, bourgeois liberals and reformers teach that exploitation will be overcome, all evils of poverty and discrimination will be eliminated, if only the "men of good will" get together, or if Christian "love of neighbor" is somehow put into practice in all areas of life. Contemporary humanists, ethical culturists, and the like, deceive others and often themselves, by taking a principle, valid under certain conditions, and then assuming that it can operate above and apart from social classes and their conflicting interests.

The dialectical interpretation of "self-interest" provides the only valid and significant explanation of working class conduct. Workers come to identify their individual and personal interests with those of their class (this is, indeed, the very meaning of class consciousness) and they can hold no good before themselves as individuals that is not contributory to the good of their class. Are they selfish or unselfish? The very asking of the question reveals its meaninglessness when applied to the struggles of the working class, the Negro people in the United States, the colonial masses everywhere. The only answer is that they are exceedingly partisan, but not for individual personal ends but for the liberation and well-being of their class or people, with which their personal ends have become completely identified.

The central point is that the classic materialists were left helpless and speechless before the fact that people can, and do, devote themselves to "ideal ends," can and do sacrifice all possible immediate ends, even their very lives, for goals which have become fully their own. And such thinkers and practical men as Helvetius and d'Holbach did this in practice while failing to recognize its possibility in theory. Most of contemporary bourgeois psychology follows this same narrow mechanistic or metaphysical line. In the words of the Soviet psychologist, E. Rubinstein, "The moral motives, which are connected with the socially significant, with duty, were completely removed from the purview of psychology, on the ground that psychology studies the real motives of conduct, while duty relates to morality, to ideology, to the sphere of the *ideal* not of the real."[17] In other words, traditional psychology, no more able to solve this problem than was the classic materialism, denies that people can be really motivated by anything other than their personal interests, and thus insists that, no matter how "unselfish" they may think they are, they are getting some kind of special "personal" satisfaction while *seeming* to sacrifice themselves for their class or their people. Freudianism has become the most extreme of all the forms of this approach, denying everything from a generous impulse to the most heroic sacrifice of all the individual's personal interests, even to life itself. Here, again, is revealed the utter bankruptcy and the inherent anti-human attitude of leading currents in bourgeois philosophy and social science.

Paralleling Freudianism, another expression of traditional individualism in ethics is found in Bertrand Russell, John Dewey, and contemporary subjective idealists generally. For them there is no possible objective moral value. Just as these people know no objective reality but only their experience or sensations, so in ethics they know no objective good but only their subjective tastes. Dewey camouflages this behind an enormous facade of "scientific method" and the like, but Russell reveals it in its unashamed nakedness. Near the end of World War II he didn't believe Hitler would succeed because "he had offended the mass of mankind too deeply," but Russell didn't think he would emulate Hitler even if he could be sure of success. And why? "Only because my desires are different from his." He continues:

> I regard the satisfaction of desire *per se* good, no matter what or whose the desire; sometimes desires are compatible, sometimes not. If A and B desire to marry each other, both can be satisfied; if each desires to murder the other without being murdered, at least one must be disappointed. Therefore marriage is better than murder, love is better than hate. This, of course, does not go to the root of the matter. Why should I think all satisfaction of desire good? Only owing to an emotion of benevolence.[18]

It would not be fair to blame this subjectivist position on classic materialism. Its roots are to be found rather in Berkeley and Hume and subjective idealism. The important point is that mechanical materialism was never able to rise above such individualism and subjectivism in theory. It could not go from the individual to society because its thinkers lived and thought in class society but dared not recognize the reality of classes. Thus there was a missing link which prevented them from moving from the individual to the social. In Marxism alone the gap is filled. Again we see how only the working class could solve a problem which had remained insoluble through the whole previous history of thought.

We are now in position to sum up something of the limitations of all non-Marxist ethical theory, whether idealist or mechanical materialist, or when it pretends to be above that, as in pragmatism and positivism. Because they ignored the fact, basic in all historical society, that people were divided into antagonistic classes, the classic moralists taught a good that was to be good for all people. The result was that it was either a good so abstract as to be good for no one, or a good for the subjection and obedience of the masses, but ignored by the rulers of society. Or it was a good for the ruling class, completely meaningless and unobtainable for the producing classes. Plato's highest moral ideal, justice, looks suspiciously like "everyone keeping in his place" and the acceptance by the masses of the rule of their "superiors." Aristotle's magnificent man was an ideal for a wealthy slave-owner, admittedly beyond the means of everyone else, while his "life of contemplation" was equally dependent on being freed from all labor by having both slaves and overseers of them. Kant's ideal man is one who obeys the "moral law" regardless of the cost to himself, his family, class, or nation.

The lesson here is that none, materialist or idealist, could accept the fact of class struggle and thus develop an ethic, a moral standard, a set of values that had any relevance to the great historic struggle of the masses of the world's exploited towards a better life. None could offer a single concrete moral goal to guide the struggle of the earth's peoples.

A number of other limitations can be noted, but they all flow from the same basic inability of the thinkers of exploiting class society to derive a genuinely all-human morality. Among these are the following dominant characteristics of past ethical thought and its systems:

(1) Individualism. For materialists this was expressed most frequently in doctrines of self-interest and the quest for personal pleasure, happiness, or well-being, as has already been discussed. For idealism it takes the form of an emphasis on the virtuous individual, or personal salvation, while ignoring the actual needs and hopes of people at large. Thus the "good man," "individual freedom," and the like are substituted for principles by which society and its institutions can be judged and evaluated.

(2) Eternality. Classic ethics could accept nothing that was not absolute and eternal as its good or governing principle. Whether the good was pleasure or happiness, or some kind of ideal of what the human personality should and could attain to, or whether it was freedom or duty, it was unchanging and unchangeable. In short, nothing that was good could change, for if it could change for the better then it wasn't good beforehand, and if it was really good it couldn't change for the worse. Materialists, to be sure, from Epicurus to Diderot, did recognize that moral judgments change in time and place, but underlying both materialist and idealist systems was the concept of an unchangeable human nature, endowed with definite fixed potentialities and equally fixed and static causes of evil and corruption. The moralists could, thereby, determine precisely what was good and bad for all time and circumstances. This utterly static metaphysical conception never appears more strikingly than in the early modern Utopias, such as those of Thomas More and Tomasso Campanella, where every slightest detail of life and culture is minutely regulated, apparently for all eternity. The most extreme expression of this metaphysical approach is seen in our own day in the writings of Aldous Huxley, for whom the very idea of time is the source of all evil.[19]

John Dewey makes a great show of criticizing this aspect of previous ethics, and in his special demagogic way he does reveal its absurdities, but only for the purpose of denying any concrete moral goal whatsoever. His whole ethical thought, in fact, is only the other side of the same picture—he so breaks up "goods," so atomizes them, that the only good is getting out of a bad situation, is movement from one state to another without any definable moral direction. Thus in place of the absolutism of the classic ethics, he substitutes an absolute relativism. The effect is even more destructive of any values or goods. If there is no standard for the objective selection among competing or contradictory goods then anything and everything is good. But history reveals with utmost clarity that times come in the affairs of men when they have to subordinate everything to the movement towards a highest good. Dewey, however, calls the belief in a *summum bonum*, or the "subordinating all aims to the accomplishment of one alone," "fanaticism."[20] This is a form of moral nihilism, that deprives mankind of moral guidance at precisely those crucial points in history when concentration on one long-range goal is indispensable for social progress. If Dewey is right, then the struggles of early Christianity, the Cromwellian and American Revolutions, our own Civil War, the October Revolution in Russia, or the common world struggle against the fascist axis were wrong.

(3) Abstractness. Both materialists and idealists were unable to escape from definitions of the moral goods or goals of mankind that were so vague, abstract, and general as to be of little or no meaning to people in the concrete conditions of life. Never do they think of food, clothing, shelter as the basic goods. Never can they really deal with the actual things that the masses of people desire and aspire to. They never thought of asking themselves the question, what do people want? They want food and shelter. But they do not want just any food or any shelter but a certain kind, depending on what they are accustomed to. They need and want a certain quantity and quality of food necessary for health and vitality. They need and want a certain quantity and quality of clothing and shelter, the nature of which is determined by a most complex set of conditions, but which no person in the world finds the slightest difficulty in describing for himself. They want health, security, love, friendship, children. They want work and recreation, the respect of their fellows, the possibility of developing special talents and capacities. They want their children to have more of all these things than they have had. Viewed abstractly, it would have been so utterly easy for any philosopher in history to have ascertained both the general direction of the desires and goals of the people and their immeasurable richness and complexity. But, due to the impact of class relations on ideology, it could never have occurred to any of them to do so.

These extraordinary, though perfectly explicable limitations of classic ethics provide a measure of the immensity of the Marxist revolution in ethical thought. Marxism utilizes the best in the classic tradition, especially the developments of the materialists in their struggle against all forms of mystical and obscurantist approaches to problems of human value. But Marxist ethics, as the ethics of the struggle for socialism, radically differs from all previous ethical schools in approach, method, and goals.

Starting with the fact that "the history of all hitherto existing society is the history of class struggles," Marxism insists that in such society there can be no such thing as an above-class ethics. The values of the various classes are determined by the relation of each to the others in the production process, and, when the relations of one class to another are antagonistic ones, their values will not only be different but in opposition. But it is necessarily the oppressed and exploited classes that generate the higher moral values, uniting as they must the larger number of people and looking towards the end of their oppression. (Higher, in moral values, is, of course, defined here not in abstract, absolutistic terms, but in terms of the whole movement of mankind towards greater mastery of the conditions of its life, as will be developed later.) Thus it was that the prophets of Israel, fighting on behalf of the people against increasing class division and stratification, and against corruption in high places, formulated so many noteworthy moral ideals. Similarly, it was not the rulers of Rome, but the down-trodden of their far-flung empire, who created the ideal of the "brotherhood of man." But not until the rise of the modern class-conscious industrial working class could the exploited clearly understand their values and formulate them scientifically. Only then, also, could they formulate the program of action through which these values could be achieved.

Thus it is that it was left to the industrial working class to achieve the first scientific materialist ethics in history. And in doing so it achieved not only an ethics for itself but for all progressive mankind: for the oppressed nations and national groups, such as the Negro people of the United States, the great peasant masses of China, India, and of all Asia, the nomadic Kurdish tribesmen of Iran, Iraq, and Turkey, the oppressed peoples of Africa and the landless Indian peasants of all Latin America. At the same time it is an ethics which alone conforms to the interests of artists and scientists, offering them not prostitution in the service of the "power elite," but a life of fruitfulness in the service of the whole people. The political and ideological leaders of the advanced capitalist nations cannot understand why hundreds of millions follow the Marxists rather than them. Class blindness, not personal stupidity, will ever prevent them from understanding why and how it is that ideals of bread, peace, democracy, socialism mean more to all workers and farmers than do ideas of "free enterprise," "private ownership," or the "sovereignty of the individual."

Marxism, in its theory of values, as in all other fields discussed in this volume, unites partisanship and objectivity. It takes its stand firmly on the needs and interests of the working class. It believes that what is good for the working class is good, period. It teaches that whatever advances the working class in class consciousness, in power, and in conditions of life is good; that whatever truly advances socialism is good. But in affirming and insisting on such partisanship to the working class, Marxist ethics never loses sight of the historic process and the future of all mankind. It takes its stand with the working class because it *is* the thought and theory of this class, and not because it feels kindly or benevolent towards the most suffering and oppressed class, as the utopian socialists did. It was the class conscious workers themselves, armed with Marxist theory, who recognized the identity of their goals with those of all progressive mankind. Their Marxist theory enabled them to recognize that theirs was the struggle for the liberation of all peoples from oppression and exploitation, for raising society to a higher level and getting rid of the exploitation of labor.

Over and over again working class experience teaches them, through struggle and adversity, what Marxist theory, as the generalized experience of the working class, also teaches. During the Civil War in the United States Marx wrote: "Labor cannot emancipate itself in the white skin where in the black it is branded." And from that time to the present, generations of American workers have had to learn from Marxist teaching, or from their own bitter experience, that unless they struggle for the civil rights of their Negro brothers, for equal pay and job opportunities, for seniority and upgrading, their own civil rights, jobs and wages suffer. Similarly, they have learned that only through the utmost solidarity in their union struggles and their active participation in politics can they achieve or even maintain decent working and living conditions. And similarly they learn the necessity for including the needs of women in their own demands and that the interests of the colonial peoples are their interests. Thus their class interests ever widen until they become the bearers of the highest and broadest interests

of the nation through their own growing proletarian interna-
tionalism and their growing awareness that their own welfare
requires peace for the whole world.

Thus Marxism, as the world outlook of the working class,
is able to unite class partisanship and the broadest human moral
ideals. In the same way the position of the working class in
society not only enables but requires it to seek the truth through
scientific investigation of all the phenomena of nature and society.
Thus, again, partisanship and objectivity constitute for the
working class a dialectical unity, just as moral objectivity in
capitalist society, without partisanship, is invariably support of
the *status quo* and is partisan to the existing ruling class. To
start with partisanship to the working class is the only basis for,
and guarantee of, both scientific and moral objectivity. Similarly,
just as the divorce of partisanship and objectivity brings the
separation of the ends men seek from the means by which they
may be realized, so does the unity of partisanship and objectivity bring with it the unity of means and ends.

The favorite and irrepressible argument raised by the bourgeois world against Marxism and Communism is that it teaches
"the end justifies the means."

In the first place it is to be seriously asked whether this question is always raised in good faith. It is often asked with malice
aforethought and represents disagreement less with the means
employed than with the ends sought. Though seldom expressed,
in previous historical epochs, in terms of "means and ends," it
was nevertheless the favorite argument of those entrenched in
power against those who sought a basic change. It was used
by the Tories against the Whigs of the American Revolution.
It was used against the Abolitionists by all who profited by or
condoned slavery. It was used against the reforms of the "New
Deal" as it is against the labor movement at every point it presents a new challenge to capitalist rule. From the old anti-labor
"conspiracy" acts to Taft-Hartley and the mis-named "right
to work" laws of the present writing, the capitalists use every
means against labor they can command and then charge labor
generally and Marxists particularly with believing "the end
justifies the means." This comes with ill-grace from those who
oppose every forward movement of the people towards a better

life, and who at the same time command all the major instruments of social power.

Secondly, partisanship without the possibility and actuality of scientific-historical objectivity, as is inevitably the case with any class that is declining because it has outlived its usefulness, leads always to expediency—any means to the end. Dark reaction, repression and torture, the destruction of all human values, is ever the instrumentality through which a decaying ruling class that can no longer maintain its rule through older established methods, seeks to prevent the rising of a new order. The Inquisition of the declining Middle Ages and the fascism of our own day bear ample and bloody witness to what happens when class partisanship is severed from any historical justification. When the end desired is an unexamined and irrational one, the means sought to promote it will be similarly blind and perverse.

On the other hand, an assumption of scientific objectivity without class partisanship must always, as long as there is class society, degenerate into pious hopes and fruitless speculation about a future that "ought to be." Necessary and desirable goals are envisioned, but without a class orientation and therefore without the required propelling power, ends are separated from means, the "good" from any manner whereby it may be achieved. This position is well illustrated by Fabian socialism or proposals for scientific social planning under capitalism. Both represent some understanding by liberals of existing evils and of goods that can and ought to be, but lacking genuine working class partisanship they are deprived of any adequate leverage in reality.

No one ever claims that any end justifies any means. To ask the question in this form clearly reveals its absurdity. As Corliss Lamont once expressed it, this would be like asking "Is the object worth the price?" And he showed that the question can never be answered until it is put specifically in terms of what the object is and what price is being asked for it.[21] The first form of the question about means and ends can never be answered, while the second or concrete form can be answered only concretely in terms of what ends justify what means. And the moment it is expressed this way it can be answered only in terms of the partisanship of given classes and the objective goods and goals they respectively seek. Any ruling class always regards the means by which it achieved its rule to be good, while it equally regards as bad all means by which its rule can be removed. The methods of fascism starkly reveal the lengths to which ruling classes go, when necessary, to maintain themselves. Their end justifies, in their minds, virtually any means, while they piously accuse the Socialist section of the world and Communists generally of teaching what they themselves practice.

With Marxism, as a science of history and society, there can be no abstract separation of means and ends from each other. The ends classes seek are determined by the form of society in which they live, primarily the existing economic relationships and the nature of state power. These same things determine, as well, the means required for these class ends to be realized. The same processes of history shape both ends and means, while these in turn are only two aspects of one and the same social movement, separable in thought but never separated in reality. The same historic process which impels working people to struggle for socialism, for the goal of peace and plenty for all mankind, requires, in the long run, that they do this through winning the majorities of individual nations and ultimately of the world as a whole to their side. This fact of itself imposes upon Marxists, as the leaders of the working class, moral requirements respecting the interests, needs, and sentiments of the great masses of people such as were never required of any preceding revolutionary class. This historic fact, of course, is not in itself a guarantee against either errors in judgment or violations of moral principles and standards of justice which socialist society seeks to advance. One cannot say today that socialism can commit no crimes or that no crimes can be committed in socialism's name. But one can argue that any such violations of fundamental moral ideals are not inherent in socialism but arise in the transition period out of particular conditions of place, time, individual leaders, historical traditions, and the like. Furthermore, they occur almost entirely in the effort to preserve the new order of society against persistent efforts to destroy it by powerful external enemies through outright aggression and every possible means of internal subversion. Such violations, however, though arising as they do out of the existing context in which the class struggle must be fought, are inimical to the cause of socialism and endanger its very success. This is the best guarantee humankind can have for the protection and advancement of its moral ideals. The final proof of this is found today in the appeal of the socialist section of the world for peaceful co-existence and competition between the two systems, against the policies advanced by the imperialists of "liberating" the peoples under socialism, "rolling back" the frontiers, and "massive retaliation" with hydrogen bombs.

The whole question of the relation of means and ends is inseparably connected with the question of the historical and scientific objectivity of Marxist working class goals. The real question is not: do Marxists believe the end justifies the means? It is rather: is it correct or not that the working class can only win its struggles for a better life, for peace and happiness, through the achievement of socialism? And, will socialism bring the liberation of mankind from all exploitation of man by man and raise all society to a higher level? Once "higher level" is defined in objective concrete terms of ever better living conditions, an ever expanding and improving material and cultural life for all the people of the world, then we have left the field of ethics and are in the area of concrete economic and political analysis.

It is impossible in such a chapter as this, or in any chapter or any book, to prove the sum-total of Marxist-Leninist principles in the inter-related realms of political economy, theory of the state, the national question, imperialism, and so on. Here we can only state what Marxism teaches concerning the comparative workings of capitalism and socialism. It finds in its analyses of these two systems the justification for its claims of the moral superiority of socialism over capitalism as well as the basis for the Marxist claim that it has achieved the objective, scientific unity of means and ends in social movement.

Marxists believe that every type of society has specific laws governing its operation. They are laws in the sense that, given a particular structure of economic relations, such and such conditions must be fulfilled if that society is to survive. Capitalism, for example, exists through the search for profits, and modern monopoly capitalism requires that its great monopoly corporations achieve the highest possible profit. This requires poverty for the majority of people, the plunder of "backward" countries, and the constant drive towards war. This incessant drive for big profits must necessarily determine the policy of the giant manufacturing corporations and at the same time of the government which they inevitably dominate. All this could not be otherwise, given these economic relations.

Just as capitalism requires exploitation and war preparation for its very existence and continuation, socialism also has its requirements, without which it would be doomed to failure and extinction. Socialism must satisfy the constantly rising material and cultural needs of all its people. It can do this only through continuous expansion of production. Unless it does this it is certain to lose out in the competition between the two worlds.

On the one side, the highest possible profits; on the other, constantly rising standards of living. The one system needs war or rumors of war; the other needs only peace and fears war as an unmitigated evil. The drive for ever greater profits brings only insecurity and impoverishment, material and cultural, to the masses. The basic economic law of socialism requires it to bring them ever more of the good things of life.

It is through such analysis of the opposed social systems of our time that Marxism believes it establishes the unity of social science and ethical values. Its moral judgments here are descriptive, yet not less moral. Its formulations are not less scientific because they bear most directly and immediately on everything that mankind in general regards as good and evil. And just as means and ends are objectively integrated so are freedom and necessity. Necessity operates equally in both societies, but in one it deprives the masses of people of all the human goods they need and desire. In the other, it succeeds only to the extent that it fulfills them. How paltry and meaningless, against such an analysis, is John Foster Dulles' talk of the "free world."

In its concept of *freedom* Marxist thought achieves its theoretical fruition and approaches the unity of theory and practice, science and ethics, nature and history. This concept of freedom is found throughout the writings of Marx and Engels. In itself, it is only an ideal towards which Marxism believes mankind must ever struggle. But, as conceived by the creators of Marxism it is an ideal that is inherent in the struggle of the oppressed and exploited for a better life and one that this struggle must not only embody but strive towards with increasing consciousness of its nature. This presents a new and revolutionary understanding of all moral values, summing them up and conceiving them in a rich and ever-expanding unity. This conception of freedom is the Marxist transformation and concretization of the ethical ideals of both the materialists and idealists through the ages. In place of a certain kind of person or life, regarded as the last word in the way of the good person or the good life, and in place of pleasure or happiness divorced from all concrete content, Marxism puts forward freedom as the all-embracing and inexhaustible good. This is the conception of a goal that is at once both relative and absolute. It seeks to give all previous moral ideals both material body and historical perspective.

All classic moral goals or ideals took human nature as something more or less fixed and final and then deduced from this abstract and static "human nature" the ideal person and the ideal life. Further they took existing forces of production and the relations built on these as equally fixed and final and imposed them as a straitjacket on all moral ideals. Marxism has no such limitations. It is thus able to present boldly an ethical ideal that is perfectly precise and scientifically measurable in the sense of direction, while in terms of content it represents mankind's own ever-developing ideals of what it can and wants to be. This is as absolute as any absolute can be in a dynamic world. It is as relative as is required by ever-developing men and women in an ever-changing society. It is sufficiently solid to be an effective guide and measuring rod. It is sufficiently flexible not to impose a straitjacket of conformity to the past on the people of the future. But can such freedom be defined in a way concrete enough to provide an ideal for people at any given stage of development and serve as a guide for their action?

The answer is that it can be so defined, and with this definition the Marxist revolution in philosophy rounds itself out. Freedom is the process of mankind's ever-increasing mastery of the conditions of its life, of people's relations to nature and to one another, for the purpose of fulfilling their needs and desires. As such it is also the process whereby, through changing nature and social relations, we humans change and develop ourselves, thus acquiring new needs, new desires, new hopes and aspirations. Marxism leaves to future men and women to determine what their desires and aspirations will be, as our ancestors have determined them in the past. Only, the freer people are from ignorance, obscurantism, exploitation, from the dead hand of the past, the freer too will they be to determine their desires objectively, with the fullest aid of scientific knowledge of themselves and of their relations to one another. The most concrete definition Marx himself ever gave of this fullest goal was "the development of human power as its own end."[22] That is to say, it is the fulfillment of our potentialities and development of our capacities as an end in itself.

Interestingly, Marx first introduced this conception of the highest level of freedom, indeed of freedom itself, after explaining the dependence of freedom on necessity. He did this in terms of the necessity to labor in order to satisfy our needs, a necessity in which freedom appears as (1) the rational organization of our relations to nature for the satisfaction of our needs, (2) the accomplishment of our goals with the least expenditure of energy, of our total life substance in the process, and (3) performing our necessary labor under conditions most worthy of our human nature. Then, on this threefold foundation, arises the freedom that consists in our human development for its own sake.

The growth of socialism in the Soviet Union has, in recent years, reached the point where it brings this last and highest level of freedom under necessity too. At the same time it widens the area of freedom rather than that of necessity. The transition from socialism to communism requires such enormous leaps in productivity, that it can come about only if and when all the members of society achieve such education and development of their capacities that they themselves can become active agents in the further growth of production. This requires shortening the working day, universal compulsory polytechnical education, improved housing, higher real wages, and so on. The moral is that the historic development of Marxist theory and practice has itself converted Marx's highest level of freedom, over and above the realm of necessity, into a necessity for further social evolution. The cultivation of the individual potentialities of all members of society as an end in itself becomes the precondition of progress.

What this means is that Marx's realm of freedom beyond necessity is part of historical necessity itself, that we achieve it not because we have been able to satisfy all our material wants, but that we are only able to satisfy our material wants through achieving it. It means that the development of our human capacities as an end in itself is not an abstract *desideratum* that might come with enormous improvement of our mastery over nature, but is a condition requisite for such mastery.

But what are such human capacities we wish to fulfill? What will future men and women want and require? What will be their standards of good people and a good life?

Engels, in his *Origin of the Family*, gives a suggestive notion of the method the Marxist employs with regard to what human needs and desires in the future might be. Speaking of the relations of the sexes and of the norms of sex behavior in future socialist society, Engels wrote:

> That will be answered when a new generation has grown up: a genera-tion of men who never in their lives have known what it is to buy a woman's surrender with money or any other social instrument of power; a generation of women who have never known what it is to give them-selves to a man from any other considerations than real love, or to refuse to give themselves to their lover from fear of the economic consequences. When these people are in the world, they will care precious little what anybody today thinks they ought to do; they will make their own practice and their corresponding public opinion about the practice of each individ-ual—and that will be the end of it.[23]

Following Engels' lead we could well ask, who are we—products of exploiting society, condoning unemployment of mil-lions in our midst, most often oblivious to the Jim-Crow raging around us, so satisfied to have our tea and coffee, bananas, rub-ber tires, gasoline and minerals, as to be unconscious of the oppression of the millions of colonial peoples involved in their attainment—who are we to determine the ideals of our descend-ants in a classless world? And who, too, are we, surrounded by the dismal ugliness of our cities, the billboards of our roadsides, the murder mysteries and sadistic movie thrillers, the advertising jingles on our radios or the vulgarity of so much of our tele-vision programs; what qualifies us to pass judgment on what free people will do and want in a world free from the exploita-tion of man by man? No, these people change themselves in the very process of fighting the exploiters and achieving their libera-tion. We witness this movement today on a colossal scale from China to Poland and Yugoslavia. And in the course of their de-veloping socialist society people will themselves create their new standards of morality and culture. And they will do it again in process of making the transition from socialism to communism.

What has just been said reveals another aspect of the Marxist concept of freedom as embracing the whole of ethics. It breaks down, for the first time, the long-honored distinction and separation of moral from *other* values, artistic, cultural, "spiritual," and what not. Just as it removes the barriers between material and what are popularly known as spiritual values (there is a difference though it has almost always been falsely drawn), it destroys any hard and fast distinction between moral and aesthetic values. For Marxism, anything that affects and influences the *quality* of human life falls in the sphere of ethics or morality, and the seriousness with which Marxists approach art is testimony to its capacity or power to influence the quality of people's lives, to make them feel and think, live and act, hope and aspire in one way rather than in another.

It is, further, an inseparable aspect of the Marxist concept of freedom that it includes breadth of human understanding, of historical perspective, scientific knowledge, and aesthetic appreciation. A would-be Marxist who disdains art and culture is not a Marxist, any more than is an artist or "cultured person" who separates art and culture from their economic and social context and the lives of the working masses. To sum up, there are no specifically moral values, aesthetic values, and so on; there are only human values with many sides or facets.

In the United States the most insistent and vehement opponent of this Marxist conception of a long-range and all-embracing ethical good is the philosophy of John Dewey. Dewey, following James, made many cogent criticisms of idealist ethics, of a good outside of time and space, of absolute and eternal moral principles, and the like. But, like James, Dewey did this not to establish a solid materialist ethics, rooted in the needs and hopes of the laboring millions, but to deny any all-inclusive ethical goal or ideal whatsoever. Following this approach one can call "good" any expedient the American imperialists may desire, anything that solves their problems of the moment, while piously teaching that Marxism holds that the end justifies the means.

Dewey's ethics is only another variant of Humeanism. There can be no denial of our knowledge of objective reality that is not accompanied by the denial of objective moral goals, by the denial of moral judgments that are more than personal taste. Dewey puts on a great show of slaying the dragon of moral absolutism—with genuine appeal to students revolting against Plato and Kant—only to introduce the more monstrous spectre of moral nihilism.

Behind Dewey's whole thought lies satisfaction with the kind of society in which he was so highly honored, and a fearful dread of revolutionary change. This lead him to deny that change can be planned as well as that it can be revolutionary. "Planned public policies," he wrote, "initiated by public authority, are sure to have consequences totally unforseeable—often the contrary of what was intended."[24] It is amusing to note that Dewey can know only one thing about the future, namely, that it will be the opposite of what we plan. In this he is like all apostles of an Unknowable who show that they must know a very great deal about something to know that it is unknowable. But what Dewey does in complex philosophical language the reactionary poet T. S. Eliot does with almost enviable simplicity. Eliot, in defining "culture," wrote: "Every change we make is tending to bring about a new civilization of the nature of which we are ignorant, and in which we should all of us be unhappy."[25]

But this leads us to one final subject, the question of the relation of freedom to necessity, another question which the whole of classic philosophy could never solve. For Dewey as for most others these concepts are utterly opposed and absolutely incompatible. If things happen necessarily in accordance with determinate laws, then men cannot be free, and contrariwise human freedom can exist only if there are no laws of individual behavior and social development. It is of the greatest historic significance that it was left for the theoreticians of the industrial working class to achieve an adequate and scientific conception of freedom and to solve the problem of its relation to necessity. It has been able to do this because it is the first class in history in the position, through its knowledge of the laws of social movement, to plan its future *freely*, and with it, the future of mankind.

Spiritualists and idealists had generally "solved" the problem of freedom by having the Creator endow man with a free will, a will that could decide anything one way or another independent of all natural causes, of all environmental influences. Pragmatists such as James and Dewey, unable to allow a miracle, achieved the same result by denying that there is any necessity in nature or society. Theirs is a world in which truly "anything can happen" and they think they have achieved human freedom by endowing the universe with their own caprice. The former, the "free-willists," took man's will out of the natural world and made it live in imaginary independence of all nature's laws. The latter, who might be called the "chance-ites" or the "fortuitous school," reduce nature to a shambles by regarding law and necessity as purely human inventions.

On the other side stood only the mechanical materialists who opposed the idealist doctrines but were prevented by their metaphysical method from understanding human freedom in its true sense. Not being able to understand its interrelation with necessity, they tended to oppose it to necessity and ended in denying any freedom altogether.

Neither side was able to grasp the real questions involved because of the classic individualist, abstract, and unhistorical method common to them. They separated the individual from his fellows and tried to find freedom for the isolated person. They sought freedom in an act of will, a choice, abstracted from the total process of the individual's reaction to and re-creation of his environment. They tried to find freedom in some realm removed from, and above, the total social process of people in their relations to one another and to nature in the course of producing the necessities of their life. They tried to find freedom in a static situation rather than in the actual process of human history.

The idealists generally sought to give each individual, on a silver platter, as a gift of the gods, what could be achieved by mankind only collectively through age-long struggles. The mechanical materialists opposed idealism but, incapable of rising above the same metaphysical limitations, tended to fall into fatalism, which is little different in practice from free will. And from this conflict emerges the third way represented by positivism and pragmatism, which once again says: "A plague on both your houses"—there is no necessity anywhere but in men's minds; anything can happen. And the third party cannot see or dares not admit that in destroying necessity, it has destroyed freedom too. For there could be no freedom in a purely fortuitous world.

It was impossible for the ideologists of exploiting classes, even under the most favorable circumstances, fully to grasp the real problems involved. This is true, even though elements of the correct answer are found in Epicurus, in Francis Bacon, in

Spinoza, Diderot, and Hegel. They could not see the question correctly because that would require seeing it in terms of collective mankind's organized and united developing mastery of all the conditions of its life. But to do that would be to repudiate the interests of every actual and potential exploiting class. Free will and fatalism are the opposite poles of a false conception of human life and its relation to nature. For the first, anything is possible if only the will chooses it. For the second, nothing we can do can possibly change the forever predetermined course of circumstances. And the Humeans swing precariously between these two impossible poles.

Neither side grasped the real question involved: Can human beings, within the limits set by their existence on this planet, collectively determine their destiny? Marxism insists that they can, and it shows theoretically how they do so and gives practical guidance in the struggle. Engels stated the theory most clearly and decisively:

> Freedom does not consist in the dream of independence of natural laws, but in the knowledge of these laws, and in the possibility this gives of systematically making them work towards definite ends. . . . Freedom therefore consists in the control over ourselves and over external nature which is founded on knowledge of natural necessity; it is therefore necessarily a product of historical development.[29]

An integral part of Marxism is the study of the methods and processes through which the working class and all oppressed and exploited mankind can emerge "from the kingdom of necessity to the kingdom of freedom."

Today, midway in the twentieth century, with one-third of mankind firmly on the socialist path, India proclaiming socialist goals, and hundreds of millions in both the capitalist and colonial countries looking for a way out of poverty and degradation, this question of freedom is no longer one of theory but one of practice and power. Two systems of society with their opposed ideologies and outlooks are competing for men's allegiance. Marxists believe that no matter how difficult the way, the laboring masses of mankind—workers, peasants, colonial peoples—will choose their freedom and will move towards it with ever clearer consciousness of their goal. This is the century of transition from the pre-history of mankind to the historic era in which the peoples of the world will plan and determine their own history.

The naive might ask, but what has this to do with ethics? The answer is that it has everything to do with ethics as the theory of mankind's quest for a better life. From the scene of brutality and exploitation, going back to the enslavement of masses of prisoners of war to build the pyramids of Egypt and the temples of Babylon, to the herding of workers into great industrial cities to man the machines that produce the steel and the instruments of industrial civilization, mankind is moving into co-operative endeavor to make the earth a garden where all may share and enjoy the fruits of their collective labor. Such a vision dwarfs the grandest moral dreams of the best prophets and thinkers of the ages. It was vouchsafed alone to the industrial working class to achieve and formulate this vision and to give the leadership necessary to convert the vision into a reality. It took the theoretical and political leaders of the modern working class to transform ethics as the ideal of a good life for a few into a program for the achievement of an ever fuller and richer life for every man, woman, and child on earth.

REFERENCE NOTES

CHAPTER 1

1. J. Maritain, *Scholasticism and Politics*, N. Y., 1940, p. 43.
2. Quoted in K. Marx, *Capital*, Vol. 1, Chicago, 1906, pp. 445f.
3. For a full analysis of this process see H. K. Wells, *Pragmatism*, N. Y., 1954.
4. B. Blanshard *et al.*, *Philosophy in American Education*, N. Y. and London, 1944, p. 5, xi.
5. B. Russell, *History of Western Philosophy*, N. Y., 1945, p. xiii.
6. W. T. Stace, *Philosophy of Hegel*, London, 1924, p. 15.
7. F. Engels, *Ludwig Feuerbach*, N. Y., 1941, p. 21.
8. A. Weber, *History of Philosophy*, N. Y., 1907, p. 1.
9. Weber, *op. cit.*, p. 3.
10. P. Frank, *Between Physics and Philosophy*, Cambridge, Mass., 1941, pp. 37f.
11. *Ibid.*, p. 146.
12. Maritain, *op. cit.*, p. 43.
13. *Ibid.*, p. 42.

CHAPTER II

1. Quoted in C. Noel, *Life of Jesus*, N. Y., 1937, p. xix.
2. K. Marx, *Capital*, Vol. I, Chicago, 1906, p. 19.
3. William James, *Pragmatism*, N. Y., 1910, p. 222.
4. B. A. G. Fuller, *History of Philosophy*, N. Y., revised ed., 1946, p. 9.
5. V. I. Lenin, *Materialism and Empirio-Criticism*, N. Y., 1954.
6. In B. Farrington, *Head and Hand in Ancient Greece*, London, 1947, pp. 28f.
7. Plato, *Republic*, Bk. iii, sect. 415.
8. Aristotle, *Metaphysics*, Bk. A. ch. 1.
9. Marx and Engels, *The German Ideology*, N. Y., 1939, p. 7.
10. F. Engels, *Dialectics of Nature*, N. Y., 1940, p. 279.
11. Marx and Engels, *op. cit.*, p. 7.
12. J. Stalin, *Dialectical and Historical Materialism*, N. Y., 1940, pp. 27f.
13. Aristotle, *loc. cit.*

14. See, for example, Leslie A. White, in *Philosophy for the Future*, Ed. Sellars et al., N. Y., 1949, pp. 357-380.

15. Marx and Engels, *op. cit.*, p. 6.

16. G. W. F. Hegel, *History of Philosophy*, Vol. I, London, 1892, pp. 53*f*.

17. Marx, *Critique of Political Economy*, Chicago, 1904, pp. 11*f*.

18. Marx and Engels, *op. cit.*, pp. 14*f*.

19. Marx, *Capital*, Vol. I, pp. 25*f*.

20. Marx and Engels, *op. cit.*, p. 35.

CHAPTER III

1. F. Engels, *Ludwig Feuerbach*, N. Y., 1941, p. 20.

2. *Ibid.*, p. 21.

3. Plato, *The Laws*, Bk. x.

4. Aristotle, *Metaphysics*, Bk. xii (Λ), ch. 8.

5. Plato, *loc. cit.*

6. La Mettrie, *Man a Machine*, Chicago, 1927, p. 3.

7. J. Stalin, *Dialectical and Historical Materialism*, p. 16.

8. J. Dewey, *The New York Times*, April 8, 1928, Sect. 9, p. 1.

9. Engels, *op. cit.*, p. 68.

10. Aristotle, *loc. cit.*

11. A. A. Luce, *Berkeley and Malebranche*, London, 1934, p. 48.

12. G. Berkeley, *Principles of Human Knowledge*, para. 96.

13. D. Hume, *Enquiry Concerning Human Understanding*, sect. 12, pt. I.

14. A. Einstein, *The Meaning of Relativity*, 3rd ed., Princeton, 1950, p. 2.

15. J. Dewey, *Quest for Certainty*, N. Y., 1929, p. 138.

16. Quoted in J. M. Keynes, *Essays in Biography*, London, 1933, p. 311.

17. D. Hume, *Dialogues Concerning Natural Religion*, in *Hume, Selections*, ed. Hendel, N. Y., 1927, p. 401.

18. J. Maritain, *Scholasticism and Politics*, N. Y., 1940, p. 42.

19. *Ibid.*, p. 48.

20. A. Schinz, *Anti-Pragmatism*, Boston, 1909, p. xv.

21. W. E. Hocking, *Types of Philosophy*, N. Y., 1929, p. 98.

22. Baron d'Holbach, *The System of Nature*, Boston, 1868, pp. 31*f*.

23. Marx, *Capital*, Vol. I, pp. 197*f*.

24. Y. H. Krikorian, ed., *Naturalism and the Human Spirit*, N. Y., 1944.

25. B. Russell, "A Free Man's Worship," in *Mysticism and Logic*, N. Y., 1918, p. 53.

26. *Ibid.*, pp. 56*f.*
27. E. Fromm, *Man for Himself*, N. Y., 1947, pp. 40*ff.*
28. Marx and Engels, *The German Ideology*, p. 36.
29. *Ibid.*, p. 30.
30. K. Marx, "On the Book of Adolph Wagner," in *Marx-Engels Archiv*, Berlin, Vol. V, pp. 387*f.*
31. F. Engels, *Dialectics of Nature*, N. Y., 1940, p. 17.
32. *Ibid.*, p. 25.
33. *Ibid.*, pp. 292*f.*

CHAPTER IV

1. Engels, *Ludwig Feuerbach*, p. 21.
2. Mao Tse-tung, *On Practice*, N. Y., n.d., p. 1.
3. Plato, *Phaedo.*
4. Aristotle, *Politics*, Bk. I, ch. 7.
5. Engels, *The Housing Question*, N. Y., pp. 29*f.*
6. Descartes, *Discourse on Method*, pt. VI.
7. Locke, J., *Essay Concerning Human Understanding*, Bk. I, ch. 1, sect. 5.
8. *Ibid.*, Bk. iv, ch. iv, sect. 3.
9. *loc. cit.*
10. Schilpp, editor, *The Philosophy of Bertrand Russell*, Evanstown and Chicago, 1944, p. 16.
11. Gassendi, "Objections to Descartes' Meditations," in *Descartes, Selections*, ed. Eaton, N. Y., n.d., pp. 229*f.*
12. Marx and Engels, *The Germany Ideology*, N. Y., 1939, p. 19.
13. Gassendi, *op. cit.*, p. 228.
14. Marx, *Capital*, Vol. I, p. 61, note.
15. Lenin, "Karl Marx," in *Selected Works*, Vol. xi, N. Y., n.d., p. 17.
16. Locke, *op. cit.*, Bk. iv, ch. xii, sect. 10.
17. Diderot, "Letter on the Blind," in *Diderot's Early Philosophical Works*, Chicago, 1916, pp. 104*f.*
18. *The New York Times*, Nov. 6, 1948.
19. *Ibid.*, Aug. 27, 1945.
20. Quoted in J. M. Keynes, *Essays in Biography*, p. 311.
21. L. Wittgenstein, *Tractatus Logico-Philosophicus*, London, 1922, pp. 197*f.*
22. B. Russell, *Human Knowledge*, N. Y., 1948, pp. 278*f.*
23. Dewey, in *Philosophy of John Dewey*, pp. 537*f.*

24. Dewey, *Problems of Men*, N. Y., 1946, pp. 195*ff*.
25. Dewey, in *Philosophy of John Dewey*, pp. 565 ff.
26. E. W. Sinnott, *American Scientist*, Jan. 1948, vol. 36, no. 1.
27. P. Frank, *Between Physics and Philosophy*, N. Y., 1941, pp. 56*f*.
28. B. Russell, *Op. Cit.*, Pt. iii, Ch. 2, "Solipsism."
29. D. Hume, *A Treatise on Human Nature*, Bk. i, Pt. iv, sec. 7.
30. Engels, *Socialism, Utopian and Scientific*, N. Y., n.d., pp. 13*ff*.
31. Luther Burbank: *His Methods and Discoveries and Their Practical Application*, ed. Whitson, John and Williams, N. Y. and London, 1915, vol. XII, p. 59.
32. See, for example, R. W. Sellars, "Some Reflections on Dialectical Materialism," in *Philosophy and Phenomenological Research*, vol. V, no. 2, Dec. 1944.
33. Sellars, "Materialism and Human Knowing," in *Philosophy for the Future*, ed. Sellars, Farber, McGill, N. Y., 1949, p. 84.
34. The reader should see Maurice Cornforth, *The Theory of Knowledge*, N. Y., 1955, for the fullest and most systematic analysis to date of the Marxist theory of knowledge.
35. Mao Tse-tung, *op. cit.*, p. 15.

CHAPTER V.

1. *N. Y. Herald Tribune*, Sept. 30, 1947.
2. *The New York Times*, Oct. 26, 1947.
3. *Ibid.*, April 28, 1946.
4. *N. Y. Herald Tribune*, Oct. 22, 1947.
5. *Ibid.*, Nov. 24, 1946.
6. See: S. Radhakrishnan, *Indian Philosophy*, London, 2nd ed., 1931, vol. i, ch. 5, for the moral content of early Indian materialism.
7. Spinoza, *Ethics*, Pt. iii, Prop. ix, note.
8. *Ibid.*, Pt. iv, Prop. xlv, note.
9. Diogenes Laertius, *Lives of Eminent Philosophers*, Bk. x, para. 132.
10. Diderot, *Interpreter of Nature; Selected Writings*, ed. Kemp, N. Y., 1938, p. 212.
11. Engels, *Ludwig Feuerbach*, p. 38.
12. Aristotle, *Nichomachean Ethics*, Bk. x, Ch. ii.
13. This question, like many others dealt with in this chapter, is treated more fully in the author's earlier work, *Socialism and Ethics*, N. Y., 1943.
14. d'Holbach, *System of Nature*, Boston, 1868, p. 111.
15. Aristotle, *op. cit.*, Bk. ix, Sect. 8.
16. T. Jefferson, *The Writings of Thomas Jefferson*, ed. Lipscomb & Bergh, Washington, 1904-05, vol. vi, p. 392.
17. E. Rubinstein, "Soviet Psychology in Wartime," *Philosophy and Phenomenological Research*, vol. 5, no. 2, Dec. 1944, p. 194.

18. B. Russell, in *The Philosophy of Bertrand Russell*, p. 194.
19. See, for example, A. Huxley, "Eternity and Time," *The American Scholar*, vol. 14, no. 3, Summer 1945.
20. J. Dewey, *Reconstruction in Philosophy*, N. Y., 1920, pp. 166, 168.
21. C. Lamont, *Humanism as a Philosophy*, N. Y., 1949, p. 282.
22. Marx, *Capital*, Chicago, 1909, vol. iii, p. 955.
23. Engels, *Origin of the Family, Private Property, and the State*, N. Y. 1942, p. 73.
24. J. Dewey, *Freedom and Culture*, New York, 1939, p. 84.
25. T. S. Eliot, *Notes Towards a Definition of Culture*, New York, 1949, p. 16.
26. Engels, *Anti-Dühring*, N. Y., 1939, p. 125.

INDEX OF NAMES

158